Comments on *Sc*

"At Vatican II, the Council access to Sacred Scripture for They exhorted all of us to learn 'the surpassing knowledge of Jesus' (Phil. 3:8), through the study of Sacred Scripture. I can think of no better introduction to this study than Scott Hahn's *Scripture Matters*."

REV. MSGR. STUART W. SWETLAND
Director, The Newman Foundation
University of Illinois

"One does not have to agree with Dr. Hahn in all particulars of *Scripture Matters* to see that he succeeds admirably in stirring things up in the world of contemporary Catholic biblical scholarship in the United States. This book should prove to be a useful stimulus for getting all of us who love Scripture to come to terms with it in our lives."

REV. JAMES SWETNAM, S.J.
Pontifical Biblical Institute, Rome

"Dr. Hahn has provided in *Scripture Matters* an invaluable series of essays that will not only help to keep students of Sacred Scripture on track, but also give them a sense of certitude concerning the Church's long-standing tradition of interpretation. After reading *Scripture Matters*, you will jump into Scripture study with a renewed zeal. Dr. Hahn's excitement for Scripture will rub off on you—get ready!"

JEFF CAVINS

SCRIPTURE
MATTERS

OTHER BOOKS BY SCOTT HAHN

Author

Understanding "Our Father":
Biblical Reflections on the Lord's Prayer
(Emmaus Road Publishing)

The Lamb's Supper: The Mass as Heaven on Earth

Hail Holy Queen:
The Mother of God in the Word of God

First Comes Love:
Finding Your Family in the Church and the Trinity

Lord, Have Mercy:
The Healing Power of Confession
(Doubleday)

A Father Who Keeps His Promises:
God's Covenant Love in Scripture
(Charis Books)

Coauthor

With Kimberly Hahn
Rome Sweet Home:
Our Journey to Catholicism
(Ignatius Press)

With Mike Aquilina
Living the Mysteries: A Guide for Unfinished Christians
(Our Sunday Visitor)

Coauthor and coeditor

Catholic for a Reason:
Scripture and the Mystery of the Family of God

Catholic for a Reason II:
Scripture and the Mystery of the Mother of God
(Emmaus Road Publishing)

General editor

The Ignatius Catholic Study Bible:
The Gospel of Matthew
The Gospel of Mark
The Gospel of Luke
The Acts of the Apostles
The Letter of St. Paul to the Romans
(Ignatius Press)

SCRIPTURE MATTERS

ESSAYS ON

READING THE BIBLE FROM THE HEART OF THE CHURCH

EMMAUS
ROAD
PUBLISHING

Steubenville, Ohio
A Division of Catholics United for the Faith

SCOTT HAHN

Foreword by Bishop Donald W. Wuerl

Emmaus Road Publishing
827 North Fourth Street
Steubenville, Ohio 43952

All rights reserved. Published 2003
Printed in the United States of America
First impression 2003

Library of Congress Control Number: 205404320
ISBN 1-931018-17-0

Cover design and layout by
Beth Hart

Cover artwork:
Sandro Botticelli, *Madonna and Child (Madonna of the Book)*

Nihil obstat: Rev. James Dunfee, *Censor Librorum*
Imprimatur: ✠ R. Daniel Conlon, D.D., J.C.D., Ph.D.
Bishop of Steubenville
October 2, 2003

To Father Michael Scanlan, T.O.R.,
a man of His Word.

Contents

CONTENTS

Foreword

The Church urges us to read the Bible, and to do so in the full context of the Church's centuries of reflecting on its meaning under the guidance of the Holy Spirit. Because God's self-revelation infinitely transcends and surpasses us, God's help is an absolute necessity if we are to expand our horizons, so limited by sin, apathy, and human nature itself. The study of the Bible, by groups or individuals, remains an occasion of God's continuous grace and enlightenment to those who avail themselves of its riches. This is why the Church so strongly urges that studying and praying from the pages of Sacred Scripture should be the lifelong project of every Christian.

Dr. Scott Hahn's love for the Word of God is enthusiastically presented in *Scripture Matters*. He has a way, which is both readable and scholarly, of inspiring his readers to discover the great treasure of Scripture. His insights and contributions to biblical scholarship in this work will not go unnoticed or unappreciated. With the touch of a master's pen, he explains some very important and yet complex concepts concerning the reliability, efficacy, meaning, and importance of Sacred Scripture for Catholics.

Those familiar with the work of Dr. Scott Hahn know that he has consistently contributed valuable insight into the meaning of Sacred Scripture. *Scripture Matters* follows in that tradition and confirms his place in today's scholarly biblical debate. It is a good book for those who are just beginning to discover the great treasure of the Word of

God, as well as for those who have already come to understand what a rich source of grace we have in the Bible.

It is easy to recommend *Scripture Matters* because, throughout the book, the deeply spiritual and profoundly scholarly work of Dr. Scott Hahn is evident. For someone who regularly turns to the pages of Sacred Scripture for spiritual nurture, or for someone who is only beginning to experience to goodness of God's Word, *Scripture Matters* is a truly enriching contribution.

The Sacred Scriptures are a precious gift of God to His people, and the priceless patrimony of the Church. They help us to know and to praise the living God. We should rejoice and thank God for the wondrous gift of God's revelation to us in Sacred Scripture. We can also be grateful for scholars such as Scott Hahn, who help us open the Scriptures in continuity with the living Tradition of the Church.

MOST REV. DONALD W. WUERL, M.A., S.T.D.
Bishop of Pittsburgh

Preface

I should not spend too many words in introducing this book. *Scripture Matters* is, after all, itself an introduction to another book: the Holy Bible. I originally wrote each of the following chapters as essays to help people to read the Bible with greater understanding and insight.

When I adapted the essays for this book, I arranged them in a certain logical sequence. The first two focus on the basic principles of reading and interpreting the Bible. The third chapter focuses on the idea of covenant, which is perhaps the most important key to understanding the Scriptures of Israel and of the Church. In chapters 4 and 5, I look to the life and work of one of history's greatest—and most misunderstood—interpreters of the Bible, Saint Thomas Aquinas. In chapter 6, I examine the biblical spirituality of a more recent saint, Josemaría Escrivá, who has had a profound influence on my own life and work.

In chapters 7, 8, 9, and 10, I try to follow the example of the great interpreters and apply the principles we've learned to certain passages of Scripture. In chapters 11 and 12, I examine some of the difficulties people encounter in reading Scripture today—especially those difficulties that are invented by scholars and pseudo-scholars.

The last two chapters take on some difficult and controversial scholarly trends, so their language is significantly more academic and technical than that of the other chapters. It's challenging, I know, but I think you will find the effort worthwhile.

The last chapter was adapted from my extended treatment of the subject, titled "Prima Scriptura," which was published in the proceedings of the Fellowship of Catholic Scholars. My conversation with Karl Keating (chapter 11) appeared first in *This Rock* magazine, and later in the *Bulletin of Applied Biblical Studies.* (My thanks to Karl for granting permission to republish the interview.) Chapter 10 appears also in *Catholic for a Reason III: Scripture and the Mystery of the Mass.* All other chapters appeared first, in some form or other, in my monthly publication that appears as an insert in *Envoy* magazine, also called *Scripture Matters.*

Well, the sooner you get into these essays, the sooner you can get out of them and into the Bible. It's my hope that you'll get much out of reading this book, but get much more out of reading the inspired Word.

SCOTT HAHN, PH.D.
Feast of Saints Cyril and Methodius, 2003

Abbreviations

Old Testament
Gen./Genesis
Ex./Exodus
Lev./Leviticus
Num./Numbers
Deut./Deuteronomy
Josh./Joshua
Judg./Judges
Ruth/Ruth
1 Sam./1 Samuel
2 Sam./2 Samuel
1 Kings/1 Kings
2 Kings/2 Kings
1 Chron./1 Chronicles
2 Chron./2 Chronicles
Ezra/Ezra
Neh./Nehemiah
Tob./Tobit
Jud./Judith
Esther/Esther
Job/Job
Ps./Psalms
Prov./Proverbs
Eccles./Ecclesiastes
Song/Song of Solomon
Wis./Wisdom
Sir./Sirach (Ecclesiasticus)
Is./Isaiah
Jer./Jeremiah
Lam./Lamentations
Bar./Baruch

Ezek./Ezekiel
Dan./Daniel
Hos./Hosea
Joel/Joel
Amos/Amos
Obad./Obadiah
Jon./Jonah
Mic./Micah
Nahum/Nahum
Hab./Habakkuk
Zeph./Zephaniah
Hag./Haggai
Zech./Zechariah
Mal./Malachi
1 Mac./1 Maccabees
2 Mac./2 Maccabees

New Testament
Mt./Matthew
Mk./Mark
Lk./Luke
Jn./John
Acts/Acts of the Apostles
Rom./Romans
1 Cor./1 Corinthians
2 Cor./2 Corinthians
Gal./Galatians
Eph./Ephesians
Phil./Philippians
Col./Colossians
1 Thess./1 Thessalonians

2 Thess./2 Thessalonians	2 Pet./2 Peter
1 Tim./1 Timothy	1 Jn./1 John
2 Tim./2 Timothy	2 Jn./2 John
Tit./Titus	3 Jn./3 John
Philem./Philemon	Jude/Jude
Heb./Hebrews	Rev./Revelation
Jas./James	(Apocalypse)
1 Pet./1 Peter	

Documents

CT   Pope John Paul II, Apostolic Exhortation on Catechesis in Our Time *Catechesi Tradendae* (October 16, 1979).

DV   Second Vatican Council, Dogmatic Constitution on Divine Revelation *Dei Verbum* (November 18, 1965).

FC   Pope John Paul II, Apostolic Exhortation on the Role of the Family in the Modern World *Familiaris Consortio* (November 22, 1981).

FR   Pope John Paul II, Encyclical Letter on the Relationship between Faith and Reason *Fides et Ratio* (September 14, 1998).

NAB   New American Bible. Washington, DC: Confraternity of Christian Doctrine, 1991, 1986, 1970.

NIV   New International Version of the Holy Bible. International Bible Society, 1973, 1978, 1984.

Chapter One

Returning to Our Senses
Reading the Bible from the Heart of the Church

Of all the books you'll ever read, the Bible is unique. Most books have only human authors. The Bible alone can truly claim to have both human authors and a divine author, the Holy Spirit.

Thus, if we want to get to God, the Bible is the one book we can't do without. Saint Jerome said that "ignorance of Scripture is ignorance of Christ."[1] And it's true: You can't understand one without the other. Jesus Christ is the Word of God incarnate, fully divine, yet fully human—like all of us, except without sin. The Bible is the Word of God inspired, fully divine yet fully human—like any other book, except without error. Both Christ and Scripture are given "for the sake of [our] salvation" (*DV*, 11).

So when we read the Bible, we need to read it on two levels at once. We read the Bible in a *literal* sense, as we read any other human literature. But we read it also in a *spiritual* sense, searching out what the Holy Spirit is trying to tell us through the words.

What the soul is to the body, the spiritual sense is to the literal. You can distinguish the two; but if you try to

---

[1] Saint Jerome, prologue to *Commentary on Isaiah*, as quoted in Second Vatican Council, Dogmatic Constitution on Divine Revelation *Dei Verbum* (November 18, 1965), no. 25 (hereafter cited in the text as *DV*).

separate them, death follows. God "has made us competent as ministers of a new covenant—not of the letter but of the Spirit; for the letter kills, but the Spirit gives life" (2 Cor. 3:6, NIV). As Saint Augustine taught, the literal sense without the spiritual is not only dead, but deadly.[2]

Before we can read the Bible's spiritual sense, we need to develop a "sacramental imagination" so that we can learn to interpret history and creation in terms of the sacred symbolism of Scripture. For God wrote the world the way men write books—to convey truth and love. Thus, nature and history are more than just created things—God fashions them as visible signs of other things, uncreated realities, which are eternal and invisible. But because of sin's blinding effects, the "book" of nature must be translated by the inspired Word of Scripture. Likewise, Scripture illuminates the spiritual significance of God's saving deeds in history—for example, the Flood or the Exodus. This is where our sacramental imagination comes in, enabling us to interpret history and creation in terms of the sacred symbolism of Scripture.

Eyes to See, Ears to Hear

You see, the deeds and the events we read in the Bible are charged with meaning. In essence, that meaning is Jesus Christ and the salvation He won for us. This is true especially of the books of the New Testament, which explicitly proclaim Jesus; but it is true as well of the books

---

[2] Cf. Saint Augustine, *On the Spirit and the Letter*, chap. 22, 23, in *Nicene and Post-Nicene Fathers*, 1st ser., vol. 5, ed. Philip Schaff (Peabody, MA: Hendrickson, 1994), 92–93 (hereafter cited as *NPNF*).

of the Old Testament, which speak of Jesus in hidden ways. The human authors of the Old Testament told as much as they were able, but they could not clearly discern the shape of all future events. However, the Divine Author—the Holy Spirit—could and did tell of the saving work of Jesus Christ, beginning with the first page of the Book of Genesis.

Thus the New Testament did not abolish the Old. Rather, the New fulfilled the Old, and in so doing, it lifted the veil from the face of the bride. Yes, the veil is beautiful; but remove the veil, and you're suddenly able to see a world charged with grandeur and sublime meaning. Water, fire, clouds, gardens, trees, hills, doves, lambs—all of these things are important details in the history and poetry of the Chosen People. But now, seen in light of Jesus Christ, they are so much more. For the Christian with eyes to see, water symbolizes the saving power of Baptism; fire, the Holy Spirit; the spotless lamb, the sacrifice of Jesus on the Cross. This is powerful. It is also personal, intended for you, as if you were the only person Jesus came to save.

Type Casting

The spiritual reading of Scripture is nothing new. The first Christians read the Bible this way. Saint Paul describes Adam as a "type" of Jesus Christ (Rom. 5:14). A *type* is a real person, place, thing, or event in the Old Testament that foreshadows something greater in the New Testament. From *type* we get the word *typology*, the study of Christ's foreshadowing in the Old Testament (cf. *Catechism*, nos. 128–30).

When men write words in order to express love, they usually resort to poetry. And in a real way, the same is true with God. Mark Twain once said, "History doesn't repeat itself, but it does rhyme." Our ears must be attuned to this divine poetry. Salvation history is a sacred mystery, conveyed in the divine poetry of Scripture. In typology, we discover God's rhyme scheme.

For instance, Saint Paul tells the story of Abraham's sons and then declares that "this is an allegory" (Gal. 4:24). He is not suggesting that the story of Abraham never really happened; he is saying that the events happened, but they pointed to something far greater.

Later in the New Testament, the tabernacle and its rituals are described in Hebrews as "types and shadows of heavenly realities" (8:5, author's translation), and the law as a "shadow of the good things to come" (10:1). Saint Peter, in turn, noted that Noah and his family "were saved through water," and that "this prefigured baptism, which saves you now" (1 Pet. 3:20–21, NAB). (Peter's word translated as "prefigured" is actually the Greek word for *typify*, or "make a type.")

Yet we need not look to the apostles alone to justify the spiritual reading of the Bible. Jesus Himself read the Old Testament this way. He referred to Jonah (Mt. 12:39), Solomon (Mt. 12:42), the Temple (Jn. 2:19), and the brazen serpent (Jn. 3:14) as "signs" that pointed to Him. We see in Luke's Gospel, as Our Lord comforted the disciples on the road to Emmaus, that "beginning with Moses and all the prophets, he interpreted to them in all the scriptures the things concerning himself" (Lk. 24:27). After this "spiritual reading" of the Old Testament, we are told, the disciples' hearts burned within them.

In imitation of Christ, the apostles continued the tradition of reading and understanding the Old Testament through the "spiritual lenses" ground by Christ. The Holy Spirit then transmitted this vision, pure and whole, to future generations through the bishops and the Fathers of the Church.

Saint Justin Martyr, for example, writing around 155, explained that the Temple sacrifices of ancient Israel were foreshadowings of the one sacrifice of Jesus Christ and its re-presentation in the liturgy: "And the offering of fine flour . . . which was prescribed to be presented on behalf of those purified from leprosy, was a type of the bread of the Eucharist, the celebration of which our Lord Jesus Christ prescribed."[3]

A More Sensible Approach

Spiritual interpretation is a science that is not just analytical, but also spiritual. And it is not just a science, but an art, one that is rooted in contemplation. Some typology is the fruit of scientific exegesis in the Spirit; other typology represents the fruit of personal contemplation. Not all types are created equal.

In order to clarify the discernment of spiritual senses, the Fathers distinguished three spiritual senses: the allegorical, moral, and anagogical. Thus, in addition to its literal sense, a given passage could also convey a *moral* truth, about how a Christian should live; an *allegorical*

[3] Saint Justin Martyr, *Dialogue with Trypho*, chap. XLI, in *Ante-Nicene Fathers*, vol. 1, eds. Alexander Roberts and James Donaldson (Peabody, MA: Hendrickson, 1994), 215 (hereafter cited as *ANF*).

truth, about the life or person of Jesus Christ; and an *anagogical* truth, about heaven. Ephrem, Athanasius, Ambrose, Jerome, Augustine, Gregory the Great, and Cassian all used spiritual exegesis to draw doctrinal and mystical riches from the Bible. Augustine went so far as to say he couldn't have become a Christian without first learning the spiritual exegesis of the Old Testament—so scandalized had he been by the wrongdoings of the Hebrew patriarchs.[4]

Of course, not all spiritual exegetes were as brilliant and artful as Augustine. Some allegorical commentary is overwrought, some is weird, and some is just plain wrong, based on mistranslations or misunderstandings of the biblical books. A few early commentators habitually applied the allegorical method to the exclusion of the literal, historical sense. This made for some unfortunate results in spiritual exegesis that flatly contradicted historical fact. Saint Thomas Aquinas spoke against such abuses when he argued for the primacy of the literal sense: "All other senses of Sacred Scripture are based on the literal."[5]

The excesses tended to give spiritual exegesis a bad name. As a result, among scholars, its popularity has had ups and downs throughout history. The twentieth century tended to be a downer, when commentators, by and large, overly concerned themselves with the literal sense of Scripture. Among some, this played out in rationalism run amok: a slavishly historical reading of the Bible,

---

[4] Cf. Saint Augustine, *Confessions*, bk. 5, chap. 11, trans. John K. Ryan (Garden City, NY: Doubleday, 1960), 128; see also Augustine, *Confessions*, bk. 6, chap. 4 and 5, 137–40.

[5] Saint Thomas Aquinas, *Summa Theologica*, I, 1, 10 *ad* 1, as quoted in the *Catechism*, no. 83.

ignoring the action of a God who transcends history. At the opposite extreme, the overemphasis of the literal became a fundamentalist pursuit of the "plain sense" of Scripture, forgetting that what seems "plain" to us moderns might seem perfectly wrong to a long-ago Israelite or Christian.

The Integral Meaning

Yet the Catholic Church has never thrown out the proverbial baby with the allegorical bathwater of some commentaries. The Church has consistently encouraged an integral reading of Scripture, which includes the literal and spiritual senses.

This integral meaning, according to Tradition, is reading Scripture as if God mattered. Or, in the gentler words of Vatican II, it's reading the Bible "with its divine authorship in mind" (*DV*, 12).

The *Catechism of the Catholic Church* unhesitatingly endorses the spiritual exegesis of the Bible: "According to an ancient tradition, one can distinguish between two senses of Scripture: the literal and the spiritual, the latter being subdivided into the allegorical, moral, and anagogical senses. The profound concordance of the four senses guarantees all its richness to the living reading of Scripture in the Church" (no. 115, emphasis omitted). The Bible in "all its richness." Now, that's some guarantee!

The *Catechism* follows up its guarantee with specifics: "By this re-reading in the Spirit of Truth, starting from Christ, the figures are unveiled [cf. 2 Cor. 3:14–16]. Thus, the flood and Noah's ark prefigured salvation by Baptism [cf. 1 Pet. 3:21], as did the cloud and the crossing of the Red Sea. Water from the rock was the figure of the spiritual gifts of Christ, and manna in the desert prefigured the Eucharist, 'the true bread from heaven' [Jn. 6:32; cf. 1 Cor. 10:1–6]" (no. 1094).

You Can Have It All!

Practically speaking, what does all this mean? Jesus wants you and me to read the Bible in its fullest sense. He wants us to see what the poet Gerard Manley Hopkins called "the dearest freshness deep down things"[6]—not just the surface beauty, though that, too, can be delightful. He wants us to have it all.

Learning to read the Bible this way means learning to read, and even to see, all over again. Yet this is not merely a technique. It's a grace, and we'll never gain it on our own steam. So we must begin with prayer. Such was the advice of Origen, the third-century Scripture scholar, who wrote that "the spiritual meaning which the law conveys is not known to all, but to those only on whom the grace of the Holy Spirit is bestowed in the word of wisdom and knowledge."[7] That's why most of the old Catholic Bibles came with the "Prayer to the Holy Spirit" printed up front.

In the Spirit, we'll learn to do more than look *at* the things of this world; together, we'll learn to look *through* them to God.

---

[6] "God's Grandeur," in *The Poems of Gerard Manley Hopkins*, eds. W. H. Gardner and N. H. Mackenzie (London: Oxford University Press, 1967), 66.
[7] Origen, preface to *De principiis*, no. 8, in *ANF*, vol. 4, eds. Alexander Roberts and James Donaldson (Peabody, MA: Hendrickson, 1994), 241.

Chapter Two

Scholars and Sense
What Makes for Good, Sound Biblical Scholarship?

In the first Father Brown mystery, "The Blue Cross,"
G. K. Chesterton's super-sleuth uncovers the archvillain
Flambeau, who had been masquerading as a Catholic
priest. Flambeau almost succeeds in fooling our hero. Then
he slips up by asking: "Ah, yes, these modern infidels
appeal to their reason; but who can look at those millions
of worlds and not feel that there may well be wonderful
universes above us where reason is utterly unreasonable?"

Father Brown responds with a decisive, "No." Later,
when he turns the criminal in to the police, he tells him
why: "You attacked reason," Father Brown says. "[That's]
bad theology."[1]

Pope John Paul II could have cited Chesterton's Father
Brown in his encyclical *Fides et Ratio* (Faith and Reason),
where he affirms that faith and reason are interdependent.
"Faith and reason 'mutually support each other.'"[2] And
later: "Faith asks that its object be understood with the
help of reason; and at the summit of its searching rea-

---

[1] G. K. Chesterton, "The Blue Cross," in *The Penguin Complete Father Brown*
(New York: Viking Penguin, 1963), 20, 23.
[2] Pope John Paul II, Encyclical Letter on the Relationship between Faith and
Reason *Fides et Ratio* (September 14, 1998), no. 55 (hereafter cited in the text
as *FR*).

son acknowledges that it cannot do without what faith presents" (*FR*, 42).

This is the vision of the Catholic Church. It is a vision for philosophy and theology, but it is also a vision for biblical interpretation. Theologians and exegetes know this from the study of the tradition, reaching back to Saint Paul and continuing through Justin Martyr, Clement of Alexandria, Augustine, and Thomas Aquinas. Faith and reason are made for each other, and there is a nuptial harmony, a marital bond of sorts, that creates their unity, interdependence, complementarity, and fruitfulness.

Extra Sensory Perception

For biblical scholars in the Catholic tradition, this interdependence of faith and reason is most evident in the tradition of the fourfold sense—that is to say, Scripture has a *literal sense* that signifies a historical reality. That historical reality then discloses three spiritual senses, traditionally identified as the allegorical sense, the tropological (or moral) sense, and the anagogical sense (cf. *Catechism*, no. 115). According to the ancient tradition of the Church, these four senses make up the integral meaning of Scripture.

The literal sense focuses on the Bible's historical events. Discerning the literal sense demands the intensive use of the scholar's reason (along with faith), as he applies the disciplines of history, linguistics, geography, and the sciences, in order to ascertain the meaning of a given biblical text.

The other three senses require faith, but these, too, employ reason. The biblical scholar can proceed in these spiritual senses only if he believes that there is a supernatural unity to the Old and New Testaments; only if he believes that all Scripture is inspired by God the Holy Spirit; and only if he believes that all Scripture is intended to advance its readers to their final end, which is heaven.

All four senses together give us what Pope John Paul II refers to as the "full sense" of Scripture, engaging both faith and reason in mutual support (cf. *FR*, 55). What applies in theology, generally is true in exegesis as well: When an exegete emphasizes either faith or reason at the expense of the other, he errs. Overemphasizing faith, he falls into fideism; overemphasizing reason, he falls into rationalism.

Pope John Paul concludes: "One should not underestimate the danger inherent in seeking to derive the truth of Sacred Scripture from the use of one method alone, ignoring the need for a more comprehensive exegesis which enables the exegete, together with the whole Church, to arrive at the full sense of the [biblical] texts" (*FR*, 55).

Unmasked!

The *Catechism of the Catholic Church* highlights Scripture's fourfold sense in several places, treating it in detail in a section titled "The senses of Scripture" (nos. 115–19). The section concludes with the Second Vatican Council's exhortation that "it is the task of exegetes to work, according to these rules [*DV* 12§3]" (no. 119). The fourfold sense, then, defines the very task of the exegete. A later article highlights the science of *typology*, which "discerns in God's works of the Old Covenant prefigurations of what he accomplished in the fullness of time in the person of his incarnate Son" (no. 128). The

Catechism does not present these methods as one optional interpretive approach among many; rather, it lays them down as interpretive norms that bind all Catholic exegetes.

Following the *Catechism*'s lead, then, Chesterton's Father Brown could surely root out a criminal disguised as a Catholic biblical scholar. A modern Flambeau might dismiss the spiritual senses of Scripture as mere flights of fancy. Or he might take a different tack and bypass the historical events of the Gospel in order to elevate their symbolic character.

Either way, Father Brown should see his cue right away to alert Valentin, "the greatest detective alive," and bring the rascal to justice.[3]

Yet would the Chesterton test work today? I'm afraid that, for many Catholic exegetes, the relationship between faith and reason is not so clear as it was for Father Brown. Within our ranks in the twentieth century, we have witnessed a great divorce, the sundering of the literal from the spiritual senses of Scripture. Exegetes who emphasize faith—and this century has produced some mighty spiritual exegetes—have sometimes retreated into a sort of fideism, abandoning the literal-historical sense to the work of specialists.

On the other hand, exegetes who pursue literal-historical research have, for the most part, bracketed off the spiritual senses. They have narrowed their focus instead, training their sights on the "historical Jesus," whom they carefully distinguish from the Christ of faith.

---

[3] Chesterton, "The Blue Cross," 22.

This is tremendously confusing. In Catholic biblical studies, many exegetes are far from the ideal set forth in *Fides et Ratio*—and they are further still from the Pontifical Biblical Commission's 1993 document *The Interpretation of the Bible in the Church*. In the introduction to that document, Pope John Paul wrote that the documents of the Magisterium, in addressing exegesis, "reject a split between the human and the divine, between scientific research and respect for the faith, between the literal sense and the spiritual sense. They thus appear to be in perfect harmony with the mystery of the incarnation."[4]

Later in the same document, we read that "exegetes have to make use of the historical-critical method. They cannot, however, accord to it a sole validity. . . . Exegetes should also explain the christological, canonical, and ecclesial meanings of the biblical texts."[5]

Notice that the Vatican has not taken the spiritual senses away from the exegete and handed them over to the theologians. No, the exegete's work must go beyond the historical and linguistic research to include the spiritual sense of the texts.

Yet, even with all the tools of modern scholarship, we still fall far short of the synthesis of our most luminary ancestors in biblical scholarship, from Jerome and Augustine, to Thomas and Hugh of Saint Victor.

---

[4] Pope John Paul II, "Address on the Interpretation of the Bible in the Church" (April 23, 1993), no. 6, in Pontifical Biblical Commission, *The Interpretation of the Bible in the Church* (Boston, MA: Pauline Books and Media, 1993), 16.
[5] Pontifical Biblical Commission, *The Interpretation of the Bible*, 106.

How did we get here? Who sundered the soul of scriptural study from its body? Let's do as our detective Father Brown would do, and reconstruct the scene of the crime.

A Tale of Two Cities

In the first centuries of the Church, there arose a similar tension, resulting from the divergent interpretive approaches of the catechetical schools of Antioch in Syria and Alexandria in Egypt. Antioch was noted for its emphasis on Scripture's literal sense, while Alexandria preferred the spiritual senses. The best of Antioch is reflected in Saint John Chrysostom's profound and eloquent exegetical sermons. At its best, the Antiochene method enabled exegetes and preachers to recreate the biblical scenes with remarkable accuracy and vividness. At Alexandria, meanwhile, the mystical interpretation of the Gospel of John predominated, aided by the allegorical method of Philo, a first-century Jewish philosopher of that city. Alexandria's depth and power are evident, for example, in the christology of Saint Athanasius, the great defender of the Trinity and the Incarnation.

Both schools, of course, had weaknesses. Both schools produced heretics. The more extreme Antiochenes tended toward rationalism, as we can see in the infamous example of Arius, the arch-heretic of the ancient Church. The excesses of Alexandria, on the other hand, tended toward the gnostic heresy, overly spiritualizing the biblical texts, even to the denial of their literal-historical meaning.

In the later patristic period, Church Fathers such as Jerome and Augustine found a balance between the two approaches, choosing from one or another to suit the needs of the moment. This balance helped to stabilize exegesis in the medieval period; while the spiritual senses predominated in the monasteries (e.g., Saint Bernard of Clairvaux), the literal received considerable attention in the universities (e.g., Saint Thomas Aquinas at the University of Paris).

Such exegesis and theological vitality coincide throughout Church history. Cardinal Newman observes at the conclusion of his study of doctrinal development: "It may be almost laid down as an historical fact that the mystical interpretation and orthodoxy will stand or fall together."[6]

Sensory Deprivation

Nevertheless, with the Protestant Reformation, spiritual exegesis gradually fell into disuse, dependent as it was upon a stable community of exegetes, who shared a common faith. Indeed, the Swiss Protestant theologian Emil Brunner identifies the unraveling of spiritual exegesis as the very substance of the Reformation: "To argue that it is right to use typology as exposition because it was used by the Apostles is an argument that . . . can only be described by the word 'terrible.' We can only warn people most urgently against this confusion of thought, which inevitably leads us back to a religious position which the Reformers had overcome; indeed, this victory constituted the Reformation."[7]

---

[6] John Henry Cardinal Newman, chap. 7, sec. 4, no. 5, *An Essay on the Development of Christian Doctrine* (Garden City, NY: Image Books, 1960), 327.
[7] Emil Brunner, *The Christian Doctrine of Creation and Redemption* (Philadelphia: Westminster, 1952), 213.

Meanwhile, in the wake of the secularist Enlightenment, historical exegesis quickly degenerated to mere "historical criticism," which turned an attitude of suspicion against the text itself. Over time, the truth of nearly every line of the Scriptures would be called into question as historical critics gained ascendancy in the universities and seminaries. Within the Church, the abuse of critical methods provoked the "modernist crisis" at the turn of the twentieth century, resulting in the excommunication of several exegetes.

Yet do these corrosive methods continue to prevail today? Let me quote from a 1985 report by Cardinal William Baum, who was then prefect of the Vatican Congregation for Catholic Education: "There is a rupture between Bible and Church, between Scripture and Tradition. . . . In the name of science, many exegetes no longer wish to interpret Scripture in the light of faith, and the end result is that doubt is cast on essential truths of faith such as the divinity of Christ and his virginal conception in the womb of Mary, the salvific and redeeming value of Christ's death, the reality of his Resurrection and of his institution of the Church. The results of this so-called scientific exegesis are being diffused in seminaries, [theological] faculties, and universities, and even among the faithful, also by means of catechesis and sometimes even in preaching. *Dei Verbum* recommended scientific exegesis, but within the bounds of faith, since the historical-scientific method alone is not sufficient in this field."[8]

---

[8] William Cardinal Baum, as quoted in Rev. Brian W. Harrison, "Pope Paul VI and the Truth of Sacred Scripture," *Living Tradition*, no. 68 (January 1997), sec. 1, italics in original.

Even in our own day, the spiritual sense remains decidedly out of fashion.

A Partial Comeback

Yet historical criticism does not tell the whole story of twentieth-century exegesis. At midcentury, in Europe, came a revival of spiritual exegesis. The *nouvelle theologie* (new theology) encouraged a return to patristic sources. This new theology found expression in the work of Henri de Lubac, Hans Urs von Balthasar, Yves Congar, Jean Daniélou, and Louis Bouyer. These men practiced spiritual exegesis as a truly critical science and spiritual art. Their movement of *ressourcement*—a return to the sources—was canonized to a certain extent by the documents of Vatican II, which repeatedly quote the Fathers as authorities.

Though I hesitate to look this gift horse in the mouth, I must admit that I often find the *nouvelle theologie* wanting for exegetical teeth. In all the great works of these great men, what is consistently missing is biblical scholarship that reaches the same heights as their insight into the mystical interpretations of the past. Perhaps the academy was not ready for such work; perhaps the entire project of *nouvelle theologie* would have stalled in the gate if these upstarts had challenged the historical-critical establishment.

Whatever the circumstances, the end results were excellent, though incomplete. Still, theirs was no small deficiency. Saint Thomas Aquinas writes that "all other senses of Sacred Scripture are based on the literal."[9] Hugh of

---

[9] Saint Thomas Aquinas, *Summa Theologica*, I, 1, 10 *ad* 1, as quoted in the *Catechism*, no. 116.

Saint Victor insisted: *"Historia fundamentum est."*[10] The literal sense is foundational. Without adequate attention to the literal-historical sense, spiritual exegesis is built on shifting sand. Unless it is set down on the concrete historical reality of the Incarnation, spiritual exegesis can easily shift into esoteric fancies.

So we who study Scripture today find ourselves in an odd predicament. Although we are the heirs of Augustine, Jerome, and Thomas, we have, for centuries, neglected our inheritance, which is nothing less than the "full sense" of God's inspired Word. Instead, we have taken a few scraps—methods, research tools, and narrow specialties—and fled to our respective corners of academia. We can view it as almost a reversal of patristic history, with historical critics retreating to their academic Antioch and *nouvelle* theologians scurrying to a latter-day Alexandria. One of the great New Testament scholars of our day, B. F. Meyer, writes, "[T]he most pressing need in biblical interpretation today is for a critical synthesis of Antioch and Alexandria."[11]

---

[10] See Groven A. Zinn, *"Historia fundamentum est:* The Role of History in the Contemplative Life according to Hugh of Saint Victor," in G. H. Shriver, ed., *Contemporary Reflections on the Medieval Christian Tradition* (Durham, NC: Duke University Press, 1974), 135–58. Zinn observes: *"Historia fundamentum est.* This phrase sums up Hugh of Saint Victor's attitude toward the role of history and the literal, historical sense of Scripture in biblical exegesis. The metaphor came from Gregory the Great's comparison of exegesis to the building of a house. The historical sense lays the foundation."
[11] B. F. Meyer, *Critical Realism and the New Testament* (Allison Park, PA: Pickwick, 1989), 33.

Letter and Spirit

Can this marriage be saved? Can we make a case for returning to our senses?

Indeed we can, and the *Catechism* does. The *Catechism of the Catholic Church* marks the first time in history that the Magisterium has endorsed the fourfold sense. It invites us to return to a method that began with Our Lord Himself. As we saw in the last chapter, Jesus spiritually interpreted the Old Testament in light of His own coming. The apostles continued this technique, and so did the apostles' successors.

Remember those words of Mark Twain: "History doesn't repeat itself, but it does rhyme." History's rhyme scheme is what we call *typology*—the science that discovers the new concealed in the old, and the old revealed in the new. Saint Thomas explained that human writers use words to signify things; but God uses even created things as signs. So not only are the *words* of Scripture signs of things that happened in history, but the *very events* were fashioned by God as material objects that show us immaterial realities—temporal events that disclose eternal verities. God writes the world as men write words.

Thus, we see the unity of the divine economy and plan for salvation history in the correlation of the literal and spiritual senses of Scripture, or in what Paul calls the "letter" and the "Spirit" (2 Cor. 3:3–18). Very similar to the two natures of Christ, the letter and spirit should be neither confused nor separated, but rather united in Christ.

The Bible as Theology

The unity of the fourfold sense is a matter of utmost importance. For Scripture is not merely raw material for theology; it *is* theology—normative and pure. As Cardinal Joseph Ratzinger has said: "The normative theologians are the authors of Holy Scripture."[12]

Scripture itself is the source and summit of theology. So when we interpret the Bible, we are not merely gathering specimens for laboratory analysis. We are recreating the inspired writers' arguments in order to find their meanings, models, assumptions, and paradigms. If we are to think God's thoughts after Him, we must think the thoughts of Matthew, Mark, Luke, and John after them.

Again, I note that this reverence for the sacred—and theological—character of Scripture is rare today. Yet it is something we must recover if we are to exercise both faith and reason, unified in a coherent Christian vision.

This is not a call to abandon historical criticism. As a tool, it is invaluable. Still, we need to recognize its particular utility and use it wisely and conscientiously. A knife can be used to cure, as in surgery, or to kill, as in an ambush. Historical criticism is the same sort of tool, and it can be used for good just as surely as it can be abused.

Notably, there are disturbing parallels between historical-critical "exclusivists" and Fundamentalists. They, too, focus only on the literal sense of the Scripture. For Fundamentalists, *sola scriptura* is the supreme rule,

---

[12] Joseph Cardinal Ratzinger, *Principles of Catholic Theology* (San Francisco: Ignatius Press, 1987), 321.

opposed to authority and tradition; Fundamentalists also exalt private interpretation of texts, opposed to any ecclesial mediation; Fundamentalists reject the spiritual senses; Fundamentalists are characterized by disdain for philosophy; and Fundamentalists often address outsiders in harsh and condescending tones. All of these attributes can be applied, though with some distinctions, to many historical critics.

Three Interpretive Criteria

What then can we do today? What can we do without?

By now, I hope it's clear that we cannot do without the fourfold sense. This principle is indispensable.

Yet certain standards must be observed to ensure that our spiritual exegesis is critically balanced and to avoid lapses into arbitrary interpretation. First, the priority of the literal-historical sense calls for careful application of literary and historical methods, including modern critical ones, "[i]n order to discover the sacred authors' intention" (*Catechism*, no. 110, emphasis omitted). Second, the uniquely inspired nature of Scripture calls for exegetes to read it "in accordance with the Spirit [cf. *DV* 12§4]," by applying three criteria set forth in the *Catechism*, echoing the words of *Dei Verbum:*

(1) "Be especially attentive 'to the content and unity of the whole Scripture'" (no. 112);
(2) "Read the Scripture within 'the living Tradition of the whole Church'" (no. 113);
(3) "Be attentive to the analogy of faith" (no. 114).

In its 1993 document, the Pontifical Biblical Commission issued additional guidelines. First, noting that "one should be especially attentive to the dynamic aspect of many texts," it warns of overly rigid applications of historical criticism: "Historical-critical exegesis has too often tended to limit the meaning of texts by tying it too rigidly to precise historical circumstances. It should seek rather to determine the direction of thought expressed by the text."[13] Second, it notes how "certain texts which in ancient times had to be thought of as hyperbole . . . must now be taken literally," particularly since "[t]he paschal event, the death and Resurrection of Jesus, has established a radically new historical context, which sheds fresh light upon the ancient texts and causes them to undergo a change in meaning."[14] Third, attention is called to the unity and convergence of literal and spiritual senses in many texts, and how spiritual exegesis was actually used by the scriptural writers themselves in both the Old and New Testaments. A fourth principle shows how to do spiritual exegesis with texts that do not explicitly affirm a spiritual sense, by looking for an "authentic doctrinal tradition or conciliar definition given to a biblical text."[15]

Thus, for example, when we read in Genesis 3:15 of the "woman" and her "seed" and the "serpent," it is right to apply a Marian interpretation—even though we cannot

---

[13] Pontifical Biblical Commission, *The Interpretation of the Bible*, 83, emphasis omitted.
[14] Pontifical Biblical Commission, *The Interpretation of the Bible*, 84.
[15] Pontifical Biblical Commission, *The Interpretation of the Bible*, 87.

find a New Testament writer who makes the connection explicitly—because we can trace a clear doctrinal tradition with conciliar definitions, thereby fulfilling the criteria given by the Pontifical Biblical Commission.

Following these magisterial guidelines, exegetes can steer a middle way between two opposite extremes: fundamentalism and corrosive criticism.

We've Only Just Begun

With the magisterial documents of recent years—and with the passing of a generation of historical critics—the tide is, at last, turning. Many prestigious scholars are beginning to discuss the limitations of historical criticism. Spiritual exegesis is making a comeback. Exegetes are rediscovering the liturgical elements in the New Testament. In fields such as apologetics and catechesis, we are witnessing a true flowering of biblical studies. In publishing, what we see is more like an explosion, with volume after volume of reprints of the Fathers and the medieval exegetes.

One fine day, historians of exegesis may, God willing, look back on a golden age of exegesis—an age that we are perhaps just beginning to see.

Chapter Three

Family Ties
If You Want to Know the Faith, Look Homeward

If you ask me what's the one key that unlocks the mysteries of faith, I won't hesitate to answer. It's the Family of God.

Think about it. Christianity is the only religion whose one God is a family. According to Pope John Paul II, "God in His deepest mystery is not a solitude, but a family, since He has in Himself fatherhood, sonship, and the essence of the family, which is love."[1]

God, then, is not like a family; He is a family. From eternity, God alone possesses the essential attributes of a family, and the Trinity alone possesses them in their perfection. Earthly households, like mine and yours, have these attributes, but only imperfectly.

Of course, Father, Son, and Holy Spirit are not "gender" terms, but relational terms. The language of the divine family is theological, not biological. The terms, rather, describe the eternal relations of the divine Persons Who dwell in communion.

---

[1] Pope John Paul II, *Puebla: A Pilgrimage of Faith* (Boston: Daughters of Saint Paul, 1979), 86.

Divinity Is as Divinity Does

The Trinity is Who God is eternally. It is His personal identity, which does not depend upon creation. Other titles—such as Lord, Lawgiver, Creator, Architect, and Physician—are metaphorical terms, describing His relationship to creatures. Only the Trinity—Father, Son, and Holy Spirit—describes God in metaphysical terms.

Yet because the Trinity reveals the deepest dimension of Who God is, it also reveals the deepest meaning of what God does. The mystery of the Trinity is "the central mystery of Christian faith and life," says the *Catechism*. "It is the mystery of God in himself. It is therefore the source of all the other mysteries of faith, the light that enlightens them" (no. 234). Thus, our understanding of God as family should also profoundly affect our understanding of all His works—of creation, redemption, and sanctification.

In short, with eyes of faith, we may discern a familial purpose in everything that exists, what the theological tradition calls "the footprints of the Trinity" *(vestigia Trinitatis).*

Reflection on the mystery of God and the mysteries of creation, then, becomes mutually enhancing. Says the *Catechism:* "The Fathers of the Church distinguish between theology *(theologia)* and economy *(oikonomia)*. 'Theology' refers to the mystery of God's inmost life within the Blessed Trinity and 'economy' to all the works by which God reveals himself and communicates his life. Through the *oikonomia*, the *theologia* is revealed to us; but conversely, the *theologia* illuminates the whole *oikonomia*. God's works reveal who he is in himself; the mystery of his inmost being enlightens our understanding of all his works" (no. 236, italics in original).

The Bible as God's Family Album

"God has left traces of his Trinitarian being in his work of creation and in his Revelation throughout the Old Testament" (*Catechism,* no. 237). The whole of the Scriptures, in fact, can be viewed as the story of how God, as Father, repeatedly strove to invite people into His household, to keep His family together, and to draw His wayward children home.

To understand the biblical and Catholic vision, however, we must first understand the culture of ancient Israel, in which the large, extended family defined the world of the individual. The family—the tribe, the clan—constituted a man's or woman's primary identity, dictating where they would live, how they would work, and whom they might marry. Often, people wore a conspicuous sign of their family identity, such as a signet ring, or had a distinguishing mark on the body.

A nation in the ancient Near East was largely a network of such families, as Israel was comprised of the twelve tribes named for Jacob's sons. Each family was unified by the bond of covenant—the wider culture's idea of what constituted human relations, rights, duties, and loyalties. When a family welcomed new members, through marriage or some other alliance, both parties—the new members and the established tribe—would seal the covenant bond, usually by solemnly swearing a sacred oath, sharing a common meal, and offering a sacrifice. The great exegete Dennis J. McCarthy, S.J. writes: "[T]he covenant between Israel and Yahweh did in fact make Israel the family of Yahweh in a very real sense . . . the result of . . . the covenant was thought of as a kind of familial relationship."[2]

God's relationship with Israel was defined by a covenant, as were His relationships with Adam, Noah, Abraham, Moses, and David. With each succeeding covenant, God opened membership in His covenant family to ever more people: first to a married couple, then to a household, then to a tribe, then to a nation, then to a kingdom—till, finally, the invitation was made universal with Jesus. Christ's "true family" consists of those who receive new birth as children of God through Baptism (cf. Jn. 3:3–8), and who do the will of the Father in heaven (cf. Mt. 12:49). They become His younger brothers (cf. Rom. 8:14–15, 29).

Sonship by Sacrament

Baptism and the Eucharist are now the means by which men and women are incorporated into God's covenant family. They mark the Christian's covenant oath, common meal, and sacrifice. The word "sacrament" itself witnesses to this truth. "Sacrament" comes from the Latin *sacramentum*, which means "oath," and the word was applied to Baptism and the Eucharist from the earliest days of the Church. The pagan Roman governor Pliny the Younger recorded that Christians in his time (the end of the first century) would gather before sunrise to sing hymns to Christ, after which they would "bind themselves by an oath."[3] This is the

---

[2] Dennis J. McCarthy, S.J., "Israel My Firstborn Son," *Way* 5 (1965): 186.

[3] *The Letters of the Younger Pliny*, bk. 10, no. 96, trans. Betty Radice (New York: Penguin Books, 1978), 294.

sacramentum, the oath, which seals the covenant: the Holy Eucharist. Jesus Himself described His relationship with the Church in explicitly covenantal terms. At the Last Supper, He blessed the cup of the new covenant in His Blood (cf. Mt. 26:28; Mk. 14:24; Lk. 22:20; 1 Cor. 11:25).

This makes a big difference in our life; for now, as Christians, we can call God "Abba! Father!" (Gal. 4:4–6). We are truly children of God (cf. Jn. 1:12; 1 Jn. 3:1–2), brothers and sisters and mothers of Christ (cf. Mk. 3:35), Who is the "first-born among many brethren" (Rom. 8:29). Christians are "members of the household of God" (Eph. 2:19). The primary revelation of Jesus Christ is God's fatherhood (cf. Jn. 15). Jesus reveals God first as Father to Himself, and then, by extension, to Christians, as "sons in the Son."[4]

The Book of Revelation makes clear that this new covenant is the closest and most intimate of family bonds. John's vision concludes with the marriage supper of the Lamb (Jesus) and the Lamb's bride (the Church). With this event—which tradition has understood as the Eucharist—Christians seal and renew their family relationship with God. With this sacrament—which is at once an oath, a sacrifice, and a covenant meal—they call God Himself their true Brother, Father, and Spouse.

The Paternal Order of Priests
This theme of family, which dominates Scripture, continues through the earliest centuries of the Church. For

---

[4] Pope John Paul II, General Audience (January 1, 1997), no. 3.

Saint Ignatius of Antioch, the divine family, the Trinity, becomes the model of concord in the Church: "Be as submissive to the bishop and to one another as Jesus Christ was to His Father, and as the Apostles were to Christ and the Father; so that there may be complete unity, in the flesh as well as the spirit." And again: "In the same way as the Lord was wholly one with the Father, and never acted independently of Him . . . so you yourselves must never act independently of your bishop and clergy."[5]

Saint Irenaeus emphasized the fatherly role of the hierarchy and of teachers.[6] Tertullian developed the notion of ecclesial motherhood, calling the Church "lady Mother."[7] For Tertullian, the Church on earth reflects the family model that is implicit in the Trinity: "Nor is even our mother the Church passed by, if, that is, in the Father and the Son is recognized the mother, from whom arises the name both of Father and Son."[8] Elsewhere, he exhorted candidates for Baptism to pray to the Father "in the house of your Mother . . . with your brethren."[9] Saint Cyprian of Carthage summarized this line of thinking with his

---

[5] Saint Ignatius of Antioch, *The Epistle to the Magnesians*, no. 13, in *Early Christian Writings* (New York: Penguin Books, 1987), 74; Saint Ignatius, *Epistle to the Magnesians*, no. 7, 72.

[6] Cf. Saint Irenaeus, *Irenaeus against the Heresies*, bk. IV, chap. XXVI, no. 2, in *ANF*, vol. 1, eds. Alexander Roberts and James Donaldson (Peabody, MA: Hendrickson, 1994), 358.

[7] Tertullian, *Ad martyras*, chap. I, trans. Rev. S. Thelwall, in *ANF*, vol. 3, eds. Alexander Roberts and James Donaldson (Peabody, MA: Hendrickson, 1994), 693.

[8] Tertullian, *On Prayer*, chap. II, trans. Rev. S. Thelwall, in *ANF*, vol. 3, 682.

[9] Tertullian, *On Baptism*, chap. XX, trans. Rev. S. Thelwall, in *ANF*, vol. 3, 679.

famous aphorism: "He can no longer have God for his Father, who has not the Church for his mother."[10]

Thus the teaching continues throughout the patristic era. It is no exaggeration to say that family imagery saturates the teachings of the Fathers of the Church. Indeed, the very title "Fathers" flows from a familial understanding of the Church.

Saint Augustine writes: "The apostles were sent as fathers; to replace those apostles, sons were born to you who were constituted bishops. . . . The Church calls them Fathers, she who gave birth to them, who placed them in the sees of their Fathers . . . such is the Catholic Church. She has given birth to sons who, through all the earth, continue the work of her first Fathers."[11]

Anybody Home?

God is a family, and Christians are His children. By establishing the new covenant, Christ founded one Church—His Mystical Body—as an extension of His Incarnation. By taking on a human body, Christ divinized flesh and, through the Church, His Mystical Body, extended the Trinity's life to all humanity. Incorporated into the Body of Christ, Christians become "sons in the Son." They become children in the eternal household of God. They share in the very life of the Trinity.

---

[10] Saint Cyprian of Carthage, *On the Unity of the Church*, no. 6, in *ANF*, vol. 5, 423.

[11] Saint Augustine, *Psalm 44, 32* as quoted in Henri de Lubac, *The Motherhood of the Church*, trans. Sergia Englund (San Francisco: Ignatius Press, 1982), 90.

The earthly household of the Trinity is the Church. This is a dominant motif in recent magisterial documents, especially the *Catechism of the Catholic Church*. The opening paragraph of the *Catechism* tells us that God "calls together all men, scattered and divided by sin, into the unity of his family, the Church" (*Catechism*, no. 1). Elsewhere, the *Catechism* says that "[t]he Church is nothing other than 'the family of God'" (no. 1655).

The Catholic Church is the universal Family of God, outside of which there is no salvation (cf. *Catechism*, no. 846). This teaching does not condemn anyone. Rather, it simply clarifies the essential meaning of salvation and the Church. Since the essence of salvation is the life of divine sonship, to speak of salvation outside of God's family, the Church, is to confuse things greatly. Being outside God's family is precisely the state of a man in need of salvation. Non-Catholic Christians are, however, considered "separated brethren," united to the family by the sacrament of Baptism. The Second Vatican Council states this truth in moving terms: "[A]ll who have been justified by faith in Baptism . . . are accepted as brothers by the children of the Catholic Church."[12]

Within the Church, as within the family, there are clearly defined roles. From the time of the apostles, the Christian faithful have viewed the clergy as spiritual fathers. Indeed, even in the Old Testament, priests were identified this way. In the Book of Judges, when the Levite

[12] Second Vatican Council, Decree on Ecumenism *Unitatis Redintegratio* (November 21, 1964), no. 3; see also *Catechism*, no. 818.

appears at Micah's door, Micah pleads, "Stay with me, and be to me a father and a priest" (Judg. 17:10). In the New Testament, Saint Paul clearly sees his role as paternal: "For I became your father in Christ Jesus through the gospel" (1 Cor. 4:15). And this attitude would continue in the early Church. Saint Jerome writes: "Be obedient to your bishop and welcome him as the father of your soul."[13] The great earthly father of the Church is, of course, the "Holy Father," the Pope.

Yet the family is not only global. It is also supremely local, in the parishes where, according to Vatican II, priests "gather together God's family as a brotherhood all of one mind."[14] Writes Pope John Paul II: "[T]he great family which is the Church . . . finds concrete expression in the diocesan and the parish family. . . . No one is without a family in this world: the Church is a home and family for everyone."[15]

Family Reunion, Saintly Communion

The Family of God model offers a more intimate experience of the Communion of Saints—as the Church's covenant family extended through time and space.

---

[13] Saint Jerome, *The Letters of Saint Jerome*, letter LII, no. 7, in *NPNF*, 2nd ser., vol. 6, eds. Philip Schaff and Henry Wace (Peabody, MA: Hendrickson, 1994), 93.

[14] Second Vatican Council, Dogmatic Constitution on the Church *Lumen Gentium* (November 21, 1964), no. 28; cf. Second Vatican Council, Decree on the Ministry and Life of Priests *Presbyterorum Ordinis* (December 7, 1965), no. 6.

[15] Pope John Paul II, Apostolic Exhortation on the Role of the Christian Family in the Modern World *Familiaris Consortio* (November 22, 1981), no. 85 (hereafter cited in the text as *FC*).

"Becoming a disciple of Jesus means accepting the invitation to belong to *God's family*" (*Catechism*, no. 2233, emphasis in original). In this context, we can understand the solicitude of the saints in heaven for the Church on earth, and we can understand the care of the Church on earth for the souls in purgatory; for the members of the Church—militant, triumphant, and suffering—are siblings in a close-knit family.

In the supernatural family of the saints, Mary, the Mother of God, holds an eminent place. Of all creatures, Mary is directly related to God by a natural bond of covenant kinship; she is the Mother of Jesus, to Whom she gave her own flesh and blood. This bond enabled mankind to share the grace of Christ by adoption. Thus, as brothers and sisters of Christ, Christians are also children of Mary, and so are bound to honor her as their mother.

Furthermore, Jesus Himself is legally bound by His Father's law ("Honor your father and your mother") to share His honor with Mary. Indeed, He fulfilled this law more perfectly than any son has ever done, by bestowing the gift of His divine glory upon Mary. Christians, then, are called to imitate Him in this way, as in all other ways.

Thus the correspondence is complete. God's family is perfect, lacking nothing. In His tender mercy, God gave Christians a mother.

At Home with the Church

The Church and the family are more than "communities"; each is, like the Trinity, a communion of persons. And so they also bear a family resemblance to one another. As the Church is a universal family, the family constitutes a "domestic Church" (cf. *Catechism*, no. 1656).

Through marriage, which is a sacrament of the New Covenant, a household receives a new family resemblance to God. Saint Paul writes: "For this reason I bow my knees before the Father, from whom every family in heaven and on earth is named" (Eph. 3:14–15). Earthly families, then, receive their "name," their identity, from God Himself.

In his "Letter to Families," Pope John Paul II writes that "the primordial model of the family is to be sought in God himself, in the Trinitarian mystery of his life. The divine 'We' is the eternal pattern of the human 'we,' especially of that 'we' formed by the man and the woman created in the divine image and likeness."[16]

Indeed, the *Catechism* goes so far as to declare: "The communion of the Holy Trinity is the source and criterion of truth in every relationship" (no. 2845). The *Catechism* then shows us how to apply this criterion: "The Christian family is a communion of persons, a sign and image of the communion of the Father and the Son in the Holy Spirit. In the procreation and education of children it reflects the Father's work of creation" (no. 2205). Within the domestic Church, all members, but especially fathers, exercise the "priesthood of the baptized" and evangelize by word and example (*Catechism*, no. 1656, emphasis omitted).

Thus, as an image of God Who is faithful and Who is One, the family bond between husband and wife must be permanent and indissoluble. Thus, too, as God is fecund

---

[16] Pope John Paul II, Letter to Families, (February 2, 1994), no. 6, emphasis omitted.

and generous, a married couple must be open to life, willing to cooperate with the Father in the conception of children. In this context, it should be clear why the Church forbids acts of contraception, abortion, homosexuality, and adultery—all of which are acts that distort the sanctity of marriage and the divine image in the family.

Further, the family is holy because Christ Himself lived in a family. The *Catechism* teaches that "Christ chose to be born and grow up in the bosom of the holy family of Joseph and Mary. The Church is nothing other than 'the family of God.' From the beginning, the core of the Church was often constituted by those who had become believers 'together with all [their] household' [cf. Acts 18:18]" (*Catechism*, no. 1655).

Prayer as a Family Matter

This understanding of God, Church, and family has profound implications for the inner life of the Christian. Grace, which by definition is "a participation in the life of God," is suddenly revealed as family life. Grace "introduces us into the intimacy of Trinitarian life: by Baptism the Christian participates in the grace of Christ. . . . As an 'adopted son' he can henceforth call God 'Father,' in union with the only Son. He receives the life of the Spirit who breathes charity into him and who forms the Church" (*Catechism*, no. 1997, emphasis omitted).

By Baptism, we are "co-heirs" with Christ and so, in the words of Saint Augustine, "Grace has gone before us; now we are given what is due. . . . Our merits are God's gifts [*Sermo* 298, 4–5: PL 38, 1367]" (*Catechism*, no. 2009, omission in original).

Among these gifts of grace is prayer, and this too we should understand in a familial way. No less an authority than the *Catechism* presents prayer in the context of covenant, communion, and family resemblance. In article 2564, we read: "Christian prayer is a covenant relationship between God and man in Christ." And elsewhere: "In the New Covenant, prayer is the living relationship of the children of God with their Father who is good beyond measure, with his Son Jesus Christ and with the Holy Spirit. The grace of the Kingdom is 'the union of the entire holy and royal Trinity . . . with the whole human spirit [Saint Gregory of Nazianzus, *Oratio*, 16, 9: PG 35, 945].' Thus, the life of prayer is the habit of being in the presence of the thrice-holy God and in communion with him" (*Catechism*, no. 2565, omission in original).

Even in its highest expressions, prayer remains, essentially, a family matter: "Contemplative prayer is a covenant relationship established by God within our hearts [cf. Jer. 31:33]. Contemplative prayer is a communion in which the Holy Trinity conforms man, the image of God, 'to his likeness'" (*Catechism*, no. 2713, emphasis omitted).

Domestic Defenses
The "Family of God" model serves contemporary Bible reading well, because exegesis sometimes degenerates into a sort of textual atomism—where passages are considered in isolation from one another and from doctrine and spirituality. But, by basing our case on scriptural texts understood in the larger framework of the Father's plan, we can raise the level of discourse, avoiding the overly defensive posture that too quickly resorts to proof-texting.

What's more, using the Family of God model, devout readers situate themselves squarely in Tradition, following the Fathers of the Church as well as recent magisterial pronouncements, most especially the *Catechism of the Catholic Church*.

Apologists find this model useful because it draws on imagery that is familiar and it explains divine truths according to a method that is positive, constructive, integral, and compelling. After all, why should we be defensive? Our best defense is a good family—and they don't get any better than the Family of God.

Chapter Four

The Angelic Doctor and the Good Book
(Or, Should Old Aquinas Be Forgot . . . ?)

The Bible made me do it.

It was my intensive study of the Scriptures—both the Old and New Testaments—that led me from an upwardly mobile career as a Protestant minister and seminary professor to the life I know today as a Roman Catholic. Every time I set out to research a particularly difficult or inscrutable passage of the Bible, I found the answer in the writings of some pope, saint, or theologian venerated by the Church of Rome.

After a long struggle, I concluded that I could only live true to the Scriptures by entering into full communion with the Catholic Church.

I recall announcing my decision to a close Catholic friend, a devoted follower of Saint Thomas Aquinas. His smile radiated his great joy at hearing the news. Yet his words stunned me. He told me that my entering the Church would be a good time to put aside all that "Yiddish lore"—meaning the Scriptures—and apply my mind to real wisdom—meaning the works of Saint Thomas.

My shock came not from any Protestant ignorance of Thomism. Indeed, it came from my reading of Saint Thomas himself, whose own commentaries on Scripture had convinced me of many of the Church's doctrines. For I had discovered the "Angelic Doctor" many years before, in a time when I was quite anti-Catholic.

A Thomist Calvinist?

When I was a sophomore at Grove City College, years before any of my theological conversions, I underwent a radical transformation in my understanding of philosophy. Perusing the college library, I'd found some books by a man named Aquinas, which I took home, devoured, and immediately began expounding to my friends. They, evangelicals all, were shocked and urged me to flee this temptation. "How can anyone be a 'Thomist Calvinist'?"

Yet I'd never read anyone like Saint Thomas—such a clear, penetrating, and deep thinker. And so I began a lifelong commitment to understanding this saint, who was not only a genius, but a man who contemplated truth and opened his soul to being, with a radical openness that I had never encountered in any teacher.

How did he get that way? I propose that Saint Thomas is best understood not simply by looking at his metaphysics, or by studying his appropriation of Aristotle, or by updating him with modern science. Rather, I suggest that Saint Thomas is fundamentally a *biblical* theologian. In fact, many of his biographers tell us that Thomas would have described himself primarily as a teacher of Scripture.

One of Thomas's earliest biographers, the Dominican Bernard Gui, has written (during Thomas's canonization process, c. 1318): "His knowledge was like an overflowing river of scriptural doctrine, sprung from the fount of Wisdom on high and then branching out through all the variety of his writings."[1]

---

[1] Bernard Gui, The 'Life of Saint Thomas Aquinas,' in Kenelm Foster, O. P., ed. and trans., *The Life of Saint Thomas Aquinas* (Baltimore: Helicon Press, 1959), 51.

Many scholars now are rediscovering the biblical depth of his teachings, and the importance of appropriating the scriptural categories that formed the framework of much of his thought. Today he is recognized by many as one of the greatest biblical theologians in history.

Hanging on Every Word

In a recent article, contemporary philosopher-theologian Michael Waldstein explains that "Scripture is the all-encompassing foundation of sacred teaching, and so it is the basis for Saint Thomas's *Summa Theologiae*."[2] As Saint Thomas himself says, "[O]ur faith receives its surety from Scripture."[3]

Why is Scripture so uniquely authoritative? Saint Thomas answers: "The author of [Sacred Scripture] is God, in whose power it is to signify His meaning, not by words only (as man also can do), *but also by things in themselves*."[4]

God "writes" the world, then, the way men write words. Thus, nature and history are more than just created things; they have more than just a literal, historical meaning. God fashions the things of the world and shapes the events of history as visible signs of other, uncreated realities, which are eternal and invisible. Saint Thomas says, "[A]s words formed by a man are signs of

---

[2] Michael M. Waldstein, "On Scripture in the *Summa Theologiae*," *The Aquinas Review* 1 (1994): 75.

[3] *The Summa Theologica of Saint Thomas Aquinas*, III, 55, 4 obj. 3, in 5 vols., trans. Fathers of the English Dominican Province (Westminster, MD: Christian Classics, 1981), also available from http://www.newadvent.org.

[4] *Summa Theologica*, I, 1, 10, emphasis added.

his intellectual knowledge; so are creatures formed by God, signs of His wisdom."[5]

But because of sin's blinding effects, the "book" of nature must be translated by the inspired Word of Scripture. Nature, since the fall, cannot be truly understood apart from Scriptures.

This is precisely the view taken in the *Catechism of the Catholic Church* (cf. nos. 112, 116), where the Magisterium refers us to the interpretive approach of Saint Thomas.

Apart from Scriptures, not even such a genius as Saint Thomas could have made much sense of God's purpose for salvation history. And the Angelic Doctor knew that.

God's Family Plan

Consider Saint Thomas's *Treatise on Law.* That treatise is interesting because, like many sections of the *Summa,* "Saint Aristotle" is quoted often. When you total up the number of quotations, however, you find that seven hundred twenty-four quotations are from Scripture and only ninety-six from Aristotle. I believe this reveals the supreme importance of Scripture in Saint Thomas's understanding of law.

Thomas deals with the meaning of law in question 90 of his *Summa Theologica.* He defines it as an ordinance of reason promulgated for the common good, made by one who has care for the community. But he goes on to explain that law is that which guides man to his end. The point is simple. We were made for God but, because of sin, we

---

[5] *Summa Theologica*, III, 12, 3 *ad* 2.

need divine assistance. Law raises God's children to the heights of Trinitarian glory.

He goes on to explain four types of law: *eternal law*, which represents God's governance of creation; *natural law*, which is man's participation in the eternal law, and through which, by our reason and by our free will, we come to know what is true and choose what is good; and *human law*, which applies the general principles of natural law to particular periods and situations for the common good of society; and *divine law*, which is revealed in all of the Old and New Testaments (cf. *Catechism*, 1950–86).

I am most interested in the fourth type, divine law, that God has revealed to us for a truly unique purpose. If the end of human law is the promotion of the common good among men, the divine law has for its purpose nothing less than our friendship with God.

Divine law is necessary for God's own fatherly purposes to be known and realized. In divine law, we discover that we were made for something greater than earthly happiness and temporal goods. We were made for the beatific vision, participation in the very life and blessedness of the Trinity for all eternity.

Our nature, however, was never enough to gain us supernatural life, even before the Fall. Original sin only made matters worse. Because of our imperfection and sinfulness, the divine law had to be delivered in two stages, the Old Law and the New Law (i.e., the Old and New Covenants).

Earthly Model, Heavenly Glory

Have you ever noticed that the Old Testament doesn't talk about the Resurrection or heaven very much, if at all?

Why not? Because in the Old Law, God gave us what we wanted—temporal welfare, prosperity, and power—in order to prepare us for the revelation of what we really needed and were made for—divine life and heavenly glory.

If diplomacy is the art of letting someone else have *your* way, then God is the consummate diplomat. Saint Thomas explains that the promises of the Old Law concern temporal goods because of sin. For God to get us back where we could attain our supernatural glory, He first had to restore a bond of trust between Himself and us. As the people of Israel attained these material goods, they discovered over time that, ultimately, the goods of earth are signs that point to the everlasting goods of heaven. Thus, Jesus came proclaiming the New Law—not merely of an earthly kingdom, but of an eternal kingdom. The Old Law is designed with our fallen human condition in mind, getting us ready for the New Law, which is given to us by Jesus Christ. The Old Law, Saint Thomas explains, is an intermediate step between the natural law and the New Law. Apart from the Old Law, man didn't know he had a supernatural end. With it, man learned he had a supernatural end to hope for, but he still lacked the means or strength to achieve it.

The New Law—the Gospel of Jesus Christ—is what delivers the power needed to help man keep both the divine law and the natural law. Saint Thomas goes so far as to identify the New Law with the indwelling of the Holy Spirit, present in the heart of the baptized believer who lives in a state of grace as a son or daughter of the living God.

Thus, for Aquinas, the New Law goes beyond the Sermon on the Mount and the other teachings of Jesus. It is nothing less than divine grace—which is divine life and power. Grace is the New Law that enables us to keep the commandments in a way that we, as children of Adam, couldn't on our own.

In his *Treatise on Law,* Thomas presents the Gospel the same way the Magisterium of the Church has presented it for two thousand years. The divine law is given in order to humble—and then exalt—us. First the Old Law humbled us and showed us our weakness, and, hence, our need for grace. Then the New Law exalted us by filling us with the Holy Spirit.

If we understand this approach, we will see how inescapable the theological dimension of law is to Saint Thomas, and how essential divine grace is for us to keep both the natural law and the New Law.

Power to Change Society

I'm convinced that many well-meaning people have fastened onto the natural law for the purpose of helping Catholics enter the American public square and discuss morality in a religiously neutral way. Surely, when we appeal to people on issues such as abortion, or capital punishment, or euthanasia, we need to appeal to the natural law; but we also need to know exactly what it is, and what is needed to keep it.

Fallen human nature is incapable of knowing the natural law with certainty. As Saint Thomas teaches, it is only possible with much effort, after a very long time. Only a few will ever come to know it, and even then with an admixture of error. If we are going to adopt the natural law tradition that our Church teaches, we should not do it with an apologetic strategy of selectivism or minimalism, because the natural law is not something that is non-religious. In drawing from the natural law tradition, we cannot escape religion.

Beyond this, divine law, according to Saint Thomas, points to the much larger framework of God's fatherly plan to raise His human family to share His divine life. Nothing less than divine life is needed to keep, at minimum, the precepts of the natural law. Saint Thomas, as I understand him, is a consistent and committed theocrat.

Therefore, the strategy of "nonreligious moral discourse" may be a betrayal of the Catholic tradition of the natural law. It is time for us to reassess the fullness of Saint Thomas's teachings and their practical implications for us today, because we must evangelize and proclaim the fullness of the Gospel.

Only in Christ will individuals receive the grace of God they need to keep the natural law—to fulfill their marital commitments, to avoid abortion, euthanasia, pornography, and so on. We must not lapse into a kind of moral semi-Pelagianism, which sees man in his fallen state—outside of a state of grace, apart from the sacraments—as being capable of establishing a just society.

I am convinced that this is a Catholic moment for our country, but it will be fulfilled only if we appropriate the fullness of the Church's teachings as explained by Saint Thomas. The task of evangelization and re-evangelization is indispensable for achieving peace and justice. But we won't have peace and justice apart from supernatural grace—which is itself a means toward a still greater end, which is personal and social holiness.

The Power behind the Tomes

We need, each and all, to return to the books that my friend called, "Yiddish lore."

Where does all this begin for the Catholic who wants to understand the Scriptures and evangelize? It begins for you and me where it began for Saint Thomas Aquinas. We begin as he did, on our knees, with Bible in hand.

Praising the habits of our hero, Bernard Gui writes:

> O wondrous mystery of Providence, that at first God conceals the meaning of His Scripture and then at last reveals it, in order to show how far short of His mysteries comes human understanding and that whoever desires the least insight into them must have recourse to Him who chose to reveal His secrets to the Prophets and the Apostles! O happy soul whose prayer was heard by God in His mercy, who thus teaches us, by this example, to possess our questioning souls in patience, so that in the study of divine things we rely chiefly on the power of prayer![6]

---

[6] Bernard Gui, as quoted in Foster, *The Life of Saint Thomas Aquinas*, 39.

Chapter Five

"Search the Scriptures"

Reading the Old Testament with Jesus, John, and Thomas Aquinas

"You search the scriptures, because you think that in them you have eternal life; and it is they that bear witness to me" (Jn. 5:39–40). Those are Jesus' words. They are recorded by Saint John in the fifth chapter of his Gospel, and illuminated by Saint Thomas Aquinas in his masterful commentary on that Gospel.

Jesus' statement is probably the most compact expression of a certain interpretive tradition that he shared with Saint John, Saint Thomas, and even the Jews to whom He spoke that day. It assumes what we would today call a *typological* reading of the Old Testament. In the words of the *Catechism:* "The Church, as early as apostolic times [cf. 1 Cor. 10:6,11; Heb. 10:1; 1 Pet. 3:21], and then constantly in her Tradition, has illuminated the unity of the divine plan in the two Testaments through typology, which discerns in God's works of the Old Covenant prefigurations of what he accomplished in the fullness of time in the person of his incarnate Son" (*Catechism*, no. 128). It assumes, in Augustine's classic phrase, that the New Testament is concealed in the Old, and the Old is revealed in the New.

What did Thomas have to say about that passage from John? "*Search the Scriptures,* that is, the Old Testament," Saint Thomas writes. "For the faith of Christ was contained in the Old Testament, but not on the surface, for it lay hidden in its depths, under shadowy symbols."[1] Thomas then goes on to identify the key that unlocks those hidden depths, the light that illumines the shadows. It is Jesus Christ. The Scriptures, he explains, "are said to be living only to the extent that they lead to . . . Christ."[2]

Jesus' statement, John's narrative, and Thomas's commentary are remarkably succinct and deceptively simple. Thus, we moderns can read them superficially and presume to understand their science of "searching the Scriptures" because, perhaps, we have a glancing knowledge of typology and the fourfold sense.

But do we really understand? And have we truly mastered the science of the ancients? Unless we understand the principles that underlie the science of typology, we cannot be sure that we have understood Thomas, or John, or Jesus when they speak of searching the Scriptures. For typology rests not on mere literary techniques, but on an implicit theology of history and, ultimately, a certain sort of sacramental metaphysics.

In this chapter, I hope to show that typological interpretation such as Saint Thomas's, which is shaped by a biblical theology, cannot proceed apart from a vision of an all-encompassing divine economy, a sacramental economy. This divine economy represents an interpretive tradition that contemporary scholarship has all but forgotten, if not rejected—a tradition shared by Thomas, John, and Jesus. It is a tradition we would do well to recover.

---

[1] Saint Thomas Aquinas, *Commentary on the Gospel of St. John*, vol. 1, no. 823, trans. J. A. Weisheipl and F. R. Larcher (Albany, NY: Magi Books, 1980), 330, emphasis in original.
[2] Aquinas, *Commentary on John*, no. 823, 330.

The Fourfold Sense

Most of us today are at least familiar with the patristic and medieval techniques of discerning Scripture's "hidden" or "shadowy" senses. It involves a unique method of reading, because the Bible is like no other book.

According to Thomas, the Bible is unique among all books because its principal author is almighty God, "in whose power it is to signify His meaning, not by words only (as man also can do), but also by things in themselves."[3] In the inspired Scripture, then, as in no other book, words signify things, but the *things* that are signified also signify other things. So historical realities—the people, places, and events of the Old Testament—signify greater spiritual realities. This outlook is echoed in the words of the *Catechism of the Catholic Church:* "Thanks to the unity of God's plan, not only the text of Scripture, but also the realities and events about which it speaks can be signs" (no. 117).

In the Bible, and only in the Bible, things that are visible, temporal, earthly, and human serve as signs of deeper mysteries that are invisible, eternal, heavenly, and divine. Thus, for example, in John's Gospel, Jesus speaks of the manna given to the Israelites as prefiguring the Eucharist (cf. Jn. 6) and the crossing of the Red Sea as foreshadowing Baptism (cf. Jn. 3).[4] The manna and the Exodus were real

---

[3] *The Summa Theologica of Saint Thomas Aquinas,* I, 1, 10, in 5 vols., trans. Fathers of the English Dominican Province (Westminster, MD: Christian Classics, 1981; also available from http://www.new advent.org.
[4] See Aquinas, *Commentary on John,* no. 954, 433.

historical events, but they also served as signs of something greater, transcendent, and supernatural.

The Bible's uniqueness calls for a unique method of interpretation, for none of the other sciences can suffice for the study of the Sacred Page. Thomas quotes a formula from Gregory the Great: "[Sacred Scripture] by the manner of its speech transcends every science, because in one and the same sentence, while it describes a fact, it reveals a mystery."[5] And so the science of biblical interpretation must enable a reader to discern multiple senses in Scripture.

According to Thomas and the tradition, the fundamental sense of Scripture is the literal sense, "whereby words signify things." The second sense is the spiritual or mystical sense, "whereby things signified by words have themselves also a signification."[6]

Thomas emphasizes that the literal sense is foundational, and that "the spiritual sense . . . is based on the literal and presupposes it."[7] The spiritual sense can never contradict or supersede the literal sense of a given biblical text: "[F]or all the senses are founded on one—the literal—from which alone can any argument be drawn, and not from those intended in allegory."[8] Moreover, "nothing necessary to faith is contained under the spiritual sense which is not elsewhere put forward by the Scripture in its literal sense."[9]

[5] *Summa Theologica*, I, 1, 10
[6] *Summa Theologica*, I, 1, 10.
[7] *Summa Theologica*, I, 1, 10.
[8] *Summa Theologica*, I, 1, 10 *ad* 1.
[9] *Summa Theologica*, I, 1, 10 *ad* 1.

Following tradition, Thomas further breaks down the spiritual sense into three senses: the *allegorical* sense, in which "things of the Old Law signify the things of the New Law"; the *moral* sense, in which actions or events "are types of what we ought to do"; and the *anagogical* sense, in which things "signify what relates to eternal glory."[10]

Consider, for example, Thomas's exegesis of the integral sense of the divine utterance, "Let there be light," in the first chapter of Genesis: "[W]hen I say, 'Let there be light,' with referring literally to corporeal light, it is to the literal sense. [If 'Let there be light'] be taken to mean 'Let Christ be born in the Church,' it pertains to the allegorical sense. But if one says, 'Let there be light,' i.e., as meaning 'Let us be conducted to glory through Christ,' it pertains to the anagogical sense. Finally, if it is said 'Let there be light,' i.e., 'Let us be illumined in mind and inflamed in heart through Christ,' it pertains to the moral sense."[11] For Saint Thomas, all the senses of the Scripture are united in Christ, and only in Christ are the Scriptures living and life-giving. Saint Thomas tells us: "[A]lthough the precepts of the old law are living, they do not contain life in themselves. They are said to be living only to the extent that they lead to . . . the Christ."[12]

In exegesis, we distinguish the four senses, not to separate them, but to unite them in the integral meaning of the text. Indeed, the literal and spiritual senses are inseparable

---

[10] *Summa Theologica*, I, 1, 10.
[11] Saint Thomas Aquinas, *Commentary of Saint Paul's Epistle to the Galatians*, trans. F. R. Larcher, O.P. (Albany, NY: Magi Books, 1966), 138.
[12] Aquinas, *Commentary on John*, no. 823, 330.

and interdependent. This is especially true and evident in certain New Testament passages in which the writer conveys a literal sense that is itself drawn from a spiritual reading of the Old Testament (cf. 1 Cor. 10:1–4).[13] Indeed, only if we see the literal and spiritual senses together can we discern the unity and integrity of the divinely intended meaning of the Scriptures.

Yet I would say that the fourfold sense, by itself, is not enough. It is an essential part of the interpretive tradition; it is something indisputably true, good, and beautiful. However, if we wish to follow Saint Thomas, it is not enough for us to merely differentiate between the literal and spiritual senses. It isn't even enough to work out a system of typology that further distinguishes the allegorical, moral, and anagogical senses.

Without a doubt, all that is indispensable; and if that's all that we accomplish in our lifetime, and if we do it with great love, we may be canonized for it. Still, even if we're canonized, we will not have gone as far as Saint Thomas in our biblical interpretation. For Thomas was more than an interpreter, more than an exegete. He was one of the Church's finest examples of a biblical theologian. This is apparent in his commentaries, and it is what enables him to be arguably the greatest systematic theologian.

There are many misconceptions about the historical shape of biblical theology, and how it differs from the

---

[13] 1 Corinthians 10:1–4 reads: "I want you to know, brethren, that our fathers were all under the cloud, and all passed through the sea, and all were baptized into Moses in the cloud and the sea, and all ate the same supernatural food and all drank the same supernatural drink. For they drank from the supernatural Rock which followed them, and the Rock was Christ."

logical order of systematic theology. It's not as if the systematic theologian is bound by logic while the biblical theologian is free to be illogical and unsystematic. Rather, the difference between them lies in their two distinct ordering principles. *Systematic theology* is based on the logical order of the various doctrines, whereas *biblical theology* is based on the chronological order of the divine economy of salvation history. In short, the biblical theologian studies the inspired narrative in order to discern the unity of God's plan in the Old and New Covenants. Through critical reflection on the canonical record of salvation history, the biblical theologian recognizes an order, a plan that reflects a divine pedagogy of God fathering his family. It's a different ordering principle, to be sure, but it is no less systematic.

In his recent dissertation, F. P. Haggard makes this important observation:

> Biblical Theology, if we may use this term to describe the primary result of Thomas' exegesis, is the attempt to grasp so far as is possible the intelligible Word of God as it is expressed by the inspired authors in the words and events of Scripture. . . . [I]t demands not merely explication of the biblical passages by means of a running commentary . . . but also to be formed into a science in the Aristotelian sense whereby conclusions about this Word are deduced from [God's] own first principles which are manifest in revelation through Scripture.[14]

---

[14] Frank Powell Haggard, "An Interpretation of Thomas Aquinas as a Biblical Theologian with Special Reference to His Systematizing of the Economy of Salvation" (Ph.D. dissertation, Drew University Press), 276.

It is this order of first principles that we call the divine economy.

The Economy

Underlying every page of Thomas's commentary is his idea of the single divine economy. We might call the divine economy the "unified field" of the sacramental worldview that is foundational to Thomas's biblical interpretation.

What is the divine economy? The word economy comes from the Greek *oikonomia*, which means the "law of the household." The divine economy, then, would be the law of God's household. The *Catechism of the Catholic Church* defines it as "all the works by which God reveals himself and communicates his life" (no. 236). Such works, for Thomas, would mean all of revelation and all of creation.

This unity holds enormous importance for his biblical interpretation. In the *Summa*, he writes: "[B]ecause Sacred Scripture considers things precisely under the formality of being divinely revealed, whatever has been divinely revealed possesses the one precise formality of the object of this science; and therefore is included under sacred doctrine as under one science."[15]

Because all of Scripture flowed from the same divine author, Thomas could treat the Bible as a single book, with a single plot; he could invoke Genesis, the Psalms, and the Song of Songs to illuminate John's Gospel.

Like any good commentator, Thomas took care to read all scriptural passages in their proper context; but, for him, the context of any Scripture must include the "content

---

[15] *Summa Theologica*, I, 1, 3.

and unity" of the whole of canonical Scripture (cf. *Catechism*, 112). The Bible *in its entirety* provided Thomas with the literal meaning that was foundational to any spiritual exegesis. And the literal meaning of the whole Bible is the historical reality of the divine economy. Thomas saw that the same God who authored Scripture also authored the world and its history, and so God invested historical events with a supernatural signification.

Thus, just as Thomas could find literary resonances between Genesis and John, he could also discern providential correlations between many Old Testament figures and Christ, between many Old Testament realities and the Church. For Thomas, these correlations aren't mere comparisons or literary echoes; and they're certainly not what the pagan Greeks called allegories. They're as real as the rain that falls, as intentional in creation as God's first *fiat*. The things signified by the words of Scripture are realities and events, but they are realities and events that signify mysteries, the supernatural mysteries of faith. Ultimately, these mysteries are what make up the divine plan and dynamic movement of history.

The linkage between the literal-historical and the spiritual senses is based upon an objective ontology of divine symbolism that is written into the very fabric of creation and into the very rhythm of salvation history. The unity of the Bible signifies a far greater unity in creation and in history. And that unity is the divine economy.

Two Testaments, Three "Days"

Thomas saw that the one, divine economy was divisible into two testaments, or "laws": the Old and the New. He also recognized how the Old Testament could be divided into two distinct periods, nature and law, both of which pointed forward to the grace of Christ in the New Covenant. Thus, Thomas spoke of three "days" of history, symbolized by Christ's first miracle at Cana, which, John tells us, occurred on "the third day." Thomas explains further: "For the first day is the time of the law of nature; the second day is the time of the written law; but the third day is the time of grace, when the incarnate Lord celebrated the marriage."[16] The three ages correspond to the time of the patriarchs, the time of the Law of Moses, and the time of the advent of Jesus Christ.

The first stage extends from the time of creation through the patriarchal period. In this age, we see a natural religion practiced in the natural family, where fathers like Noah and Abraham fulfill priestly and kingly roles by virtue of their paternity. The family table is a natural altar; the family meal a natural sacrifice. But Genesis also shows how sin progressively dismantles this natural way.

So the period of nature gave way to written law—the time of animal sacrifice, the laws of Moses, a separate sanctuary, the Levitical priesthood, ritual purity, and Israel's separation from the Gentiles. Yet this era, too, fell short of God's promise.

The period of grace arrives with the advent of Jesus Christ, the Son of God, and the establishment of the Church and the sacraments of the New Testament. This age will remain until the consummation of history.

---

[16] Aquinas, *Commentary on John*, no. 338, 150.

In this tripartite division of nature, law, and grace, Thomas discerned God's gradual revelation of his glory. In his *Commentary on John*, Thomas works this out in a simple but profound way in his treatment of water. In the age of nature, water was a natural sacrament, "suggested in the first production of things, when the Spirit of God hovered over the waters."[17] Indeed, water remains even now a natural sacrament of cleanness, simply because it cleanses.

In the age of law, water afforded "a spiritual regeneration," Thomas says, "but it was imperfect and symbolic." This occurred during the Exodus from Egypt, when the waters parted and the Israelites passed through the Red Sea. "Accordingly," Thomas adds, "they did see the mysteries of the kingdom of God, but only symbolically, 'seeing from afar' (Heb. 11:13)."[18]

In the age of grace, the figure of water receives its "efficacy from the power of the incarnate Word,"[19] and, through Baptism, man is born "of water and the Holy Spirit" (Jn. 3:5) into eternal life. With Christ comes the fulfillment of the types in the sacraments of the New Testament. It is only through Christ that we can search the Scriptures, and see the meaning of the types.

In this sequence, Thomas sees a divine pedagogy that respects human nature and human ways of knowing. Indeed, water is not only necessary for human life, but, according to Thomas, "for the sake of human knowledge." As Thomas writes:

---

[17] Aquinas, *Commentary on John*, no. 443, 188.
[18] Aquinas, *Commentary on John*, no. 443, 185, citation in original
[19] Aquinas, *Commentary on John*, no. 443, 188.

For, as Dionysius says, divine wisdom so disposes all things that it provides for each thing according to its nature. Now it is natural for man to know; and so it is fitting that spiritual things be conferred on man in such a way that he may know them . . . . But the natural manner of this knowledge is that man knows spiritual things by means of sensible things, since all our knowledge begins in sense knowledge. Therefore, in order that we might understand what is spiritual in our regeneration, it was fitting that there be in it something sensible and material.[20]

In other words, throughout the ages of nature and law, God taught us as only God can, using things to signify greater things. In the fullness of time, however—in the third age, the age of grace—He sent His only Son. Still, in the age of grace, man continues to know spiritual things by means of sensible signs, or sacraments. Thus, Thomas often speaks of sacraments of the Old Testament and sacraments of the New. In both the old and new sacraments, a divine truth is mediated to man through sensible signs. In the age of grace, "we see the kingdom of God and the mysteries of eternal salvation"—and therein lies the difference—but still we see them "imperfectly."[21]

It is when we pass from the final period of history, the state of grace, into the eternal state of glory that man may see divine things as they are, without their sacramental veils. In heaven, Thomas says, "there is perfect regeneration . . . because we will be renewed both inwardly and

---

[20] Aquinas, *Commentary on John*, no. 443, 188.
[21] Aquinas, *Commentary on John*, no. 433, 185.

outwardly. And therefore we shall see the kingdom of God in a most perfect way."[22] What will we "see" when God removes the sacramental veils of material water? According to Thomas, water ultimately "signifies the grace of the Holy Spirit . . . the unfailing fountain from whom all gifts of grace flow."[23]

Thus, Thomas demonstrates that water has served as a sacrament since the beginning of creation, that it undergoes a partial disclosure in the age of law, and that these types find fulfillment in the age of grace. Only in glory, however, may man gaze upon the reality signified by the sacraments. Only in heaven is the "living water" manifested apart from the sacramental veils—as the glory of the Spirit of God (cf. Rev. 22:1, 2; Jn. 7:37–39).

What applies to water applies to the other sacraments as well. Thomas provides another useful illustration of the "three ages" in his discussion of the Bread of Life discourse in John 6. Bread has always provided sustenance for man in the order of nature; yet, in its "natural" state, it also prefigured the unleavened bread of the Passover and the manna that rained down in the desert; these in turn served as foreshadowing types of the Holy Eucharist. Thomas explains: "[E]ach is a symbol of the spiritual food. But they are different because [the manna] was only a symbol; while the other [the bread of the Christians] contains that of which it is the symbol, that is, Christ himself."[24] Through these three successive ages of the divine econo-

---

[22] Aquinas, *Commentary on John,* no. 433, 185.
[23] Aquinas, *Commentary on John,* no. 577, 239.
[24] Aquinas, *Commentary on John,* no. 954, 379.

my—nature, law, and grace—God drew increasingly nearer to man. With the sacraments of the New Law, God united Himself to man. But only in heaven will the glory of that union be fully perfected and unveiled to us. That is the moment for which Thomas prayed, and toward which all creation groans. In the words of "Adoro Te Devote": "O Jesus, whom I now see veiled, / when shall my longing prayer be blest, / that I may see your face unveiled / and in that glorious vision rest?"[25]

Conclusion

Behind Thomas's biblical commentary, then, is one divine economy, two laws (or covenants), and three ages of salvation history. It is on this foundation—one, two, and three—that Thomas can interpret the four senses in a coherent and systematic way. Again, this is no mere hermeneutic. John Boyle has pointed out—in his under-stated way—that "Thomas has little to say of a strictly hermeneutical nature. This may be because Thomas is more interested in actually interpreting Scripture than in thinking about interpreting Scripture."[26]

That's true enough, and it speaks volumes about the difference between Thomas's approach to Scripture and that of many modern scholars. For the heirs of Descartes and Kant, being is elusive, and knowing is everything. So they think endlessly about thinking about the Scriptures, and read endlessly about reading the Scriptures. For

---

[25] "Adoro Te Devote," author's translation.
[26] John F. Boyle, "Saint Thomas Aquinas and Sacred Scripture," *Pro Ecclesia* 4, no. 1 (1995): 95.

Thomas, however, being was the object, and it was knowable. Moderns produce hermeneutics. The ancients produced metaphysics. But the greatest medievals, like Thomas, described a divine economy, a sacramental economy of creation and revelation—which itself bore witness to what we might call a sacramental hermeneutic and a sacramental metaphysics.

For Thomas, the Sacred Page is charged with the grandeur of God, and the world itself is a sign of transcendent realities. Typology tells the spiritual meaning of history, and that meaning is the divine economy, in which we see a rich divine causality at work in time and space. The world of the four senses is a real world. It is the world in which we live and move and search the Scriptures.

Chapter Six

Passionately Loving the Word
Putting Scripture to Work with Saint Josemaría

The world knows Josemaría Escrivá (1902–75) best as the founder of Opus Dei and the Priestly Society of the Holy Cross. Members of the Catholic Church know him best for his personal holiness and intercessory power. This powerful witness led to his recognition by the universal Church on October 6, 2002, when Pope John Paul II canonized Josemaría Escrivá, declaring him worthy of public veneration and imitation.

Yet neither we, nor the Church, nor the world, can fully understand the accomplishments of Saint Josemaría, or the graces he received, until we have first come to understand his use of the Scriptures. For, in Opus Dei, he worked out a thoroughly biblical spirituality; and he saw the institution as built on solidly scriptural foundations. In perhaps the most powerful precis of his spirituality, his homily "Passionately Loving the World," Saint Josemaría repeatedly claims the Bible as his primary witness: "This doctrine of Sacred Scripture, as you know, is to be found in the very core of the spirit of Opus Dei." And also: "This I have been teaching all the time, using words from holy Scripture."[1]

---

[1] Saint Josemaría Escrivá, *In Love with the Church* (New York: Scepter, 1989), no. 54, 52. This and other works of Saint Josemaría also available at http://www.escrivaworks.org.

Indeed, I would go so far as to say that the Bible always served as Saint Josemaría's primary referential language. Though he was steeped in the teachings of the Fathers and Doctors of the Church, was fluent in scholastic theology, and kept current with trends in contemporary theology, it was to Scripture that he returned again and again in his preaching and writing, and it was to Scripture that he directed his spiritual children in Opus Dei.

He saw clearly the unity of the two Testaments, the Old and the New. The Old Testament oracles did not lose relevance for Saint Josemaría just because they had been fulfilled in the New. Rather, they shone with a new and more brilliant light. He did not hesitate to hold up the patriarchs and prophets of Israel as spiritual exemplars for Christians today: "When you receive Our Lord in the Holy Eucharist, thank him from the bottom of your heart for being so good as to be with you. Have you ever stopped to consider that it took centuries and centuries before the Messiah came? All those patriarchs and prophets praying together with the whole people of Israel: Come, Lord, the land is parched! If only your loving expectation were like this."[2]

Saint Josemaría quoted frequently from both the Old and New Testaments, but especially from the Gospels, to which Tradition has assigned a preeminent place (cf. *DV*, 18). Perhaps no phrases appear so often in his writings and homilies as those that invoke the Sacred Page:

---

[2] Saint Josemaría Escrivá, *The Forge* (New York: Scepter, 1987), no. 99.

"as the Gospel tells us," "as the Gospel advises," "Sacred Scripture tells us," "the Gospels relate," "remember the Gospel story . . . ."

According to Bishop Alvaro del Portillo, who was Saint Josemaría's companion, confessor, and successor in the direction of Opus Dei: "I was myself always impressed with the facility with which he could cite from memory exact phrases from the Holy Bible. Even during everyday conversations, he would often take a starting point from some pertinent text in order to inspire us to a more profound prayer. He lived on the word of God."[3]

Scripture as a Measure

The founding of Opus Dei took place on October 2, 1928, when Saint Josemaría "saw" the Work of God (as yet unnamed) as a way of sanctification in daily work and in the fulfillment of the Christian's ordinary duties.

What did Opus Dei look like at that moment? We do not know the visual details, but we can glimpse the Work incarnate in the later writings of the founder. There, he spoke of the Scriptures as a reliable measure of his way of life, which was "as old as the Gospel but, like the Gospel, ever new."[4] At the beginning of his seminal work, *The Way*, he writes: "How I wish your bearing and conversation were such that, on seeing or hearing you, people

---

[3] Most Rev. Alvaro del Portillo, as quoted in Cesare Cavalleri, ed., *Immersed in God: Blessed Josemaría Escrivá, Founder of Opus Dei, as Seen by His Successor, Bishop Alvaro del Portillo* (New York: Scepter, 1996), 121.

[4] Saint Josemaría Escrivá, as quoted in Congregation for the Causes of Saints, *Decree Cause of Canonization* (April 9, 1990); http://www.ewtn.com.

would say: This man reads the life of Jesus Christ."[5] Conversely, in discussing those who do not live Christian charity, Saint Josemaría said, "They seem not to have read the Gospel."[6]

His own reading of the Gospel, and of Scripture in general, was illuminated by his particular foundational charism, which led him to develop ideas that had been passed over in previous theology. He is notable for his novel or renewed emphasis on certain notions found in the Scriptures: the universal call to holiness, for example, and the sanctification of ordinary life. Again and again, he was drawn to contemplate the Gospels' tantalizing allusions to Jesus' thirty years of hidden life. Even in these relative silences, he found a model for the "hidden life" of ordinary people working in the world.

Study of the Scripture, then, was essential to his personal spirituality and to the program he developed for members of Opus Dei. He assumed that Scripture not only enabled readers to know Jesus, but also empowered them to imitate Him. "In our own life we must reproduce Christ's life. We need to come to know him by reading and meditating on Scripture."[7]

His Method

Saint Josemaría practiced and preached a particular way to approach the Scriptures in prayer. His way is intensive rather than exhaustive. Bishop del Portillo recalled that the

---

[5] Saint Josemaría Escrivá, *The Way* (New York: Scepter, 1992), no. 2.
[6] Saint Josemaría Escrivá, *Furrow* (New York: Scepter, 1992), no. 26.
[7] Saint Josemariá Escrivá, *Christ Is Passing By*, (New York: Scepter, 1974), no. 14.

founder "gave constant proof of an extraordinary veneration for Sacred Scripture. The Holy Bible, together with the tradition of the Church, was the source from which he ceaselessly drew for his personal prayer and preaching. Every day he read some pages—about a chapter—of Scripture, generally from the New Testament."[8]

This practice of daily study of the New Testament—about five minutes' time—Saint Josemaría prescribed to all those whom he directed. He urged them, when they read, to enter imaginatively into the biblical scenes, assuming the role of one of the characters or a bystander. "I advised you to read the New Testament and to enter into each scene and take part in it, as one more of the characters. The minutes you spend in this way each day enable you to *incarnate* the Gospel, reflect it in your life and help others to reflect it."[9]

Elsewhere, he developed the idea further, again emphasizing the imaginative effort as an almost sensory experience: "Make it a habit to mingle with the characters who appear in the New Testament. Capture the flavor of those moving scenes where the Master performs works that are both divine and human, and tells us, with human and divine touches, the wonderful story of his pardon for us and his enduring Love for his children. Those foretastes of Heaven are renewed today, for the Gospel is always true: we can feel, we can sense, we can even say we touch God's protection with our own hands."[10]

---

[8] Most Rev. del Portillo, as quoted in Cavalleri, *Immersed in God*, 119.
[9] Escrivá, *Furrow*, no. 672, emphasis added; see also Saint Josemaría Escrivá, Friends of God (New York: Scepter, 1997), no. 222.
[10] Escrivá, *Friends of God*, 216.

The Power to Transform

Though his actual reading took only five minutes per day, we must not confine Saint Josemaría's meditation on Scripture to those few moments. He also prayed the Scriptures in his daily Mass and in his recitation of the Divine Office. He frequently used biblical commentaries of the Fathers of the Church for spiritual reading. Indeed, he insisted that a Christian's personal meditation on Scripture must feed his mental prayer as well as the spontaneous prayer that fills his entire day. "For we do need to know it well, to have it in our heart and mind, so that at any time, without any book, we can close our eyes and contemplate [Christ's] life, watching it like a movie. In this way the words and actions of our Lord will come to mind in all the different circumstances of our life."[11]

With the reading of Scripture, then, comes the grace of transformation, of conversion. Reading the Bible is not a passive act, but an active seeking and finding. "If we do this without holding back, Christ's words will enter deep into our soul and will really change us. For 'the word of God is living and active, sharper than any two-edged sword, piercing to the division of the soul and spirit, of joints and marrow, and discerning the thoughts and intentions of the heart' (Heb. 4:12)."[12]

Divine Filiation and the Revealed Word

At the heart of Opus Dei is a single idea. Said Saint Josemaría: "[D]ivine filiation is the basis of the spirit of

---

[11] Escrivá, *Christ Is Passing By*, no. 89.
[12] Escrivá, *Christ Is Passing By*, no. 89, citation in original.

Opus Dei. All men are children of God."[13] One day in 1931, Saint Josemaría experienced his own divine sonship mystically, while riding a streetcar in Madrid. At that moment, he felt "in an explicit, clear, definitive way, the reality" of being a child of God, and he left the streetcar babbling, *"Abba, Pater! Abba, Pater!"* (cf. Gal. 4:6).[14]

That experience had a profound influence on his subsequent thinking, preaching, writing, and prayer. All Christian doctrine, he believed, can and should be considered in light of this truth. But we find a most powerful example of God's fatherly care in the inspiration of Scripture. Indeed, divine filiation is the essential point uniting all of the Bible. Salvation history is the story of God's fatherly plan for bestowing divine sonship on all men.

Many Fathers of the Church, most notably Saint John Chrysostom, spoke of God's revelation in terms of "accommodation" and "condescension," which Chrysostom understood as fatherly actions.[15] In order to reveal Himself, God *accommodates* Himself to man, just as a human father stoops down to look his children in the eye. As a human father will sometimes resort to "baby talk," God sometimes communicates by *condescension*—that is, He speaks as humans would speak, in the language of humans, as

---

[13] Escrivá, *Christ Is Passing By*, no. 64.
[14] Andrés Vázquez de Prada, *The Founder of Opus Dei: The Life of Josemaría Escrivá*, Volume I: The Early Years (New York: Scepter, 2001), 295–96.
[15] See discussion in Stephen D. Benin, *The Footprints of God: Divine Accommodation in Jewish and Christian Thought* (Albany: State University of New York Press, 1993).

if He had the same passions and weaknesses. Thus, in Scripture, we read of God "repenting" His decisions, when surely God is never in need of repentance.

Yet human fathers do not only stoop down to their children's level. They also raise their children up to function on an adult level. In a similar way, God also, at times, communicates by *elevation*—that is, He lifts His children up to a divine level, endowing merely human words with divine power (as in the case of the prophets).

Relying on God's fatherly care, Saint Josemaría trusted the word of Scripture as he would trust the words of his father. His filial confidence is exemplary of the timeless Christian belief:

> [T]he books of both the Old and New Testaments *in their entirety, with all their parts*, are sacred and canonical because written under the inspiration of the Holy Spirit, they have God as their author . . . . Therefore, since everything asserted by the inspired authors or sacred writers must be held to be asserted by the Holy Spirit, it follows that the books of Scripture must be acknowledged as teaching solidly, faithfully, and without error that truth which God wanted put into sacred writings for the sake of salvation (*DV*, 11, emphasis added).

Bishop del Portillo recalled that Saint Josemaría exuded confidence in the divine origin of the holy Scriptures, not only when he preached and wrote, but also in his everyday conversation. "One sign of his reverence for Sacred Scripture was his habit of introducing his quotations with the words 'The Holy Spirit says . . . .' It was not just a manner of speaking; it was a heartfelt act of faith which helped us really feel the eternal validity of, and the solid weight of truth behind, expressions which might otherwise have sounded overly familiar."[16]

Literal and Spiritual Senses

Saint Josemaría placed tremendous emphasis on the imaginative assimilation of small details of the Gospel narratives. No word was superfluous for him; no detail so small as to lack significance. In his view, the Holy Spirit did not waste words.

Yet his care for the literal-historical sense did not render him blind to the Scripture's "spiritual sense." For the Church has traditionally interpreted the biblical texts as both *literally* true and as *spiritual* signs of Christ, of heaven, or of moral truths (cf. *Catechism*, nos. 115–17). Indeed, though Saint Josemaría never himself employed the terminology of "literal exegesis" or "spiritual exegesis," he stands as one of the great spiritual exegetes of his time. I agree with Cardinal Parente, who observed that Saint Josemaría's commentaries on Sacred Scripture reflected a "profundity and immediacy often superior even to that found in the works of the Fathers of the Church."[17]

Here, I could multiply examples. Consider this compact teaching from *The Way:* "Like the good sons of Noah, throw the mantle of charity over the defects you see in your father, the Priest."[18] Saint Josemaría evokes the scene of Noah's shameful drunkenness (cf. Gen. 9:20–23) and draws out a stunning moral teaching for contemporary life

---

[16] Most Rev. del Portillo, as quoted in Cavalleri, *Immersed in God,* 121.
[17] Most Rev. Pietro Parente, as quoted in Cavalleri, *Immersed in God,* 121.
[18] Escrivá, *The Way,* no. 75.

in the Church. This is spiritual exegesis at its most concise and incisive. In a single line, we learn from our Old Testament ancestors why we should never spread scandal about a member of the clergy, who in faith we call "Father."

We see another striking example of the founder's spiritual exegesis when he compares the sins of Christians to the biblical Esau's willingness to exchange his birthright for a bowl of lentils (cf. Gen. 25:29–34). For a moment's pleasure, such Christians are willing to alienate themselves from God and even forsake heaven altogether.[19]

Saint Josemaría did not hesitate to actualize the biblical text by applying it to contemporary life, and here he stands in the line of great exegetes from Saint Augustine and Saint John Chrysostom to Saint Anthony of Padua and Jacques Bossuet. Scholars call this extensive interpretation the "accommodated spiritual sense."

Still, none of these spiritual insights supersedes the literal-historical truth of the biblical text, which Saint Josemaría revered. In the words of Saint Thomas Aquinas, "All other senses of Sacred Scripture are based on the literal."[20]

Thus, to lay a firm foundation, Saint Josemaría made careful studies of what biblical science had to say about the cultural milieux of ancient Israel and the Roman Empire in the time of Jesus. His preaching on Christ's passion, for example, shows that he was familiar with historical scholarship on Roman methods of crucifixion.

[19] He uses this image of Esau in several places. Cf. Escrivá, *Friends of God*, no. 13.
[20] Saint Thomas Aquinas, *Summa Theologica*, I, 1, 10 *ad* 1, as quoted in *Catechism*, no. 116.

His homilies on Saint Joseph display a keen interest not only in philology, but also in the customs of ancient Jewish family life and labor.

Occasionally, Saint Josemaría received extraordinary, divine illuminations revealing a particular spiritual sense of a biblical text. While saying Mass on the feast of the Transfiguration in 1931, he received this mystical insight:

> When I raised the host there was *another voice*, without the sound of speech. A voice, perfectly clear as always, said, *Et ego, si exaltatus fuero a terra, omnia traham ad me ipsum!* ["And I, when I am lifted up from the earth, will draw all things to myself" (1 Jn. 12:32)]. And here is what I mean by this: I am not saying it in the sense in which it is said in Scripture. I say it to you meaning that you should put me at the pinnacle of all human activities, so that in every place in the world there will be Christians with a dedication that is personal and totally free— Christians who will be other Christs.[21]

This sudden insight had a profound influence on the subsequent development of Opus Dei. Surely, it came from God. As always, grace builds on nature and perfects it. What Saint Josemaría describes is clearly an instance of infused contemplation—but one that is firmly based on a sustained and disciplined *life* of biblical meditation.

I can think of few anecdotes that so perfectly illustrate this principle sketched out by the Pontifical Biblical Commission in its 1993 document *The Interpretation of the Bible in the Church:* "[I]t is above all through the liturgy

---

[21] Saint Josemaría Escrivá, as quoted in Prada, *The Founder of Opus Dei*, 287.

that Christians come into contact with Scripture . . . . In principle, the liturgy, and especially the sacramental liturgy, the high point of which is the eucharistic celebration, brings about the most perfect actualization of the biblical texts . . . . Christ is then 'present in his word, because it is he himself who speaks when Sacred Scripture is read in the Church' (*Sacrosanctum Concilium*, 7). Written text thus becomes living word."[22]

Text and Context

Saint Josemaría studied the Scriptures earnestly. He knew, however, that the Bible was not a self-evident or self-interpreting text. And, though God sometimes gave him supernatural lights, the founder knew that these were extraordinary phenomena—certainly not the usual way of coming to understand a text.

If he could not rely on his own lights, nor depend exclusively on mystical phenomena, where did he habitually turn in the ordinary course of his biblical studies? He looked to the Church and her living Tradition, to which the ancient Fathers are "always timely witnesses" (*Catechism*, no. 688). A cursory glance at any volume of his homilies will reveal his intimate familiarity with the works of Jerome, Basil, Augustine, and Thomas Aquinas.

Saint Josemaría tested all his scriptural insights—even those he believed to be divinely inspired—against the witness of the Fathers and the papal and conciliar Magisterium. For he well knew the dangers that lurked in an over-reliance

---

[22] Pontifical Biblical Commission, *Interpretation of the Bible in the Church*, pt. IV, sect. C, no. 1 (Boston, MA: Pauline Books & Media, 1993), 124.

on private interpretation of the Scriptures. Indeed, he found a clear warning on the matter in the very pages of the Scriptures! On the first Sunday of Lent, 1952, he reflected on the subtle ways Satan tempted Jesus in the desert:

> It's worth thinking about the method Satan uses with our Lord Jesus Christ: he argues with texts from the sacred books, twisting and distorting their meaning in a blasphemous way. Jesus doesn't let himself be deceived: the Word made flesh knows well the divine word, written for the salvation of men—not their confusion and downfall. So, we can conclude that anyone who is united to Jesus Christ through Love will never be deceived by manipulation of the holy Scripture, for he knows that it is typical of the devil to try to confuse the christian conscience, juggling with the very words of eternal wisdom, trying to turn light into darkness.[23]

We may conclude from the current Babel of conflicting biblical interpretations that Satan's methods have not changed much over the millennia. Amid such confusion, Saint Josemaría stands out as a model of intelligent yet childlike faith. While many Christian exegetes spent the twentieth century retreating into agnosticism and irrelevance, Saint Josemaría thrived on a complete and critically informed confidence in the Bible and in the Church as its infallible interpreter.

We can see, touch, and study his legacy in the Navarre Bible project, which he inspired. Initiated in the early

---

[23] Escrivá, *Christ Is Passing By*, no. 63.

1970s at the University of Navarre in Spain, the Navarre Bible offers a reliable and beautiful translation of the Scriptures, supplemented by ample quotations from the Church councils, Fathers, and Doctors. This project has done much to enable non-theologians and non-ecclesiastics to enjoy the Bible as Saint Josemaría did, and to be enriched by it as he was.

The Place of the Bible

Saint Josemaría's most profound encounters with Sacred Scripture came not in his study or even in his oratory pew, but in the liturgy. Like the Fathers of the Second Vatican Council, he saw the Mass as the encounter *par excellence* with Jesus Christ in "bread and word."[24] The Holy Mass, within which is found the Liturgy of the Word, is, for Saint Josemaría, the "root and center" of interior life.

His homilies—which are saturated with quotations and allusions from both Testaments of the Bible—always find their focus in the liturgical season, and specifically in the readings of the day. Indeed, he saw the Mass as the supernatural habitat of his homilies:

> You have just been listening to the solemn reading of the two texts of Sacred Scripture for the Mass of the twenty-first Sunday after Pentecost. Having heard the Word of God you are already in the right atmosphere for the words I want to address to you: words of a priest, spoken to a large family of the children of God in his Holy

---

[24] Cf. Escrivá, *Christ Is Passing By*, nos. 116, 118, 122; cf. Escrivá, *The Forge*, no. 437.

Church. Words, therefore, which are intended to be supernatural, proclaiming the greatness of God and his mercies towards men; words to prepare you for today's great celebration of the Eucharist.[25]

Like the Fathers of the Church and the Fathers of the Second Vatican Council, Saint Josemaría looked upon the Mass as a particularly graced moment for receiving the Word of God. The inspirations received in the Liturgy of the Word should be profound and lasting: "We now listen to the word of Scripture, the epistle and the gospel—light from the Holy Spirit, who speaks through human voices so as to make our intellect come to know and contemplate, to strengthen our will and make our desire for action effective."[26]

The Virtuous Interpreter

In canonizing Josemaría Escrivá, the Church has held him up as worthy of imitation. There can be no doubt that such imitation must include intensive study, disciplined prayer, and meditative reading of the Scriptures. His own daily program witnessed to this. The "norms of piety" he followed, and which he bequeathed to his children in Opus Dei, are saturated with biblical quotations.

What is clearly central for him, however, is the encounter and identification with Jesus Christ, to the point of becoming *"ipse Christus,"* Christ Himself. This goal must be attained through certain determinate means, among

---

[25] Escrivá, *In Love with the Church*, no. 51.
[26] Escrivá, *Christ Is Passing By*, no. 89.

them the meditative reading of the Gospels. Thus, one cannot understand or live the vocation to Opus Dei without at least aspiring to a high degree of biblical fluency.

Though he lived most of his life before the Second Vatican Council, Saint Josemaría anticipated much of its teaching—certainly, at least, its emphasis on the universal call to holiness and apostolate, which had been a hallmark of Opus Dei since 1928. I believe, however, that he was especially attuned to the Church's doctrines on Sacred Scripture—its truth, authority, inspiration, and inerrancy—which found such robust expression in the Council's Dogmatic Constitution on Divine Revelation, *Dei Verbum*.

As many laymen tend to see their wives' best qualities described in the "virtuous woman" of Proverbs 31, so I tend to see Saint Josemaría, who is a spiritual father to me, in the words of *Dei Verbum* 25. There, the Council Fathers offer their vision of the ideal priest. As I conclude, I would be so bold as to adapt their words to describe Saint Josemaría and so many of the priests who have followed him in Opus Dei and in the Priestly Society of the Holy Cross.

They "hold fast to Sacred Scriptures through diligent sacred reading and careful study."

They take care "so that none of them will become an 'empty preacher of the word of God outwardly, who is not a listener to it inwardly.'"

They "share the abundant wealth of the divine word with the faithful committed to them, especially in the sacred liturgy."

They "learn by frequent reading of the divine Scriptures the 'excellent knowledge of Jesus Christ' (Phil. 3:8)."

They "gladly put themselves in touch with the sacred text itself, whether it be through the liturgy, rich in the divine word, or through devotional reading, or through instruction."

And they "remember that prayer should accompany the reading of Sacred Scripture, so that God and man may talk together"; for, in the words of Saint Ambrose, "we speak to him when we pray; we hear him when we read the divine saying" (*DV*, 25).

Chapter Seven

Going on Vocation
Why Fathers Are Priests and Priests Are Fathers

To my six children, I am a father. What does that mean to them? It means that I provide for them. I give them a name, a home, and food to sustain them. I teach them, guide them, and discipline them. I love them unconditionally; I forgive them for the trouble they cause. I pray for them daily.

In short, I am a priest in my home.

For I give my family what my pastor gives his parishioners. He provides us a home in the church, and spiritual sustenance in the Eucharist. He gives us a name in Baptism. He forgives our sins in Confession; he teaches, guides and disciplines. Every day, he intercedes for us.

In short, he is a father in the Church.

One of the marvels of God's plan is that He has given fathers a priesthood and priests a fatherhood. Within the family, the father stands before God as a priest and mediator. Within the Church, the priest stands before his parish as a father.

This is a powerful truth. And it is more than a metaphor. It is something profoundly sacramental, and built into the fabric of God's plan—from the very beginning.

The Rising Son

In studying the Old Testament, we can divide the history of the priesthood into two periods: the patriarchal and the Levitical. The patriarchal period corresponds to the Book of Genesis, while the Levitical period begins in Exodus, and lasts until the coming of Jesus Christ.

The religion of the patriarchal period was significantly different from the religion practiced by Israel after Moses received the Law on Mount Sinai. Patriarchal religion was firmly based on the natural family order, most especially the authority handed down from father to son—ideally the firstborn—often in the form of the "blessing" (cf. Gen. 27).

In the entire Book of Genesis, we find no separate priestly institution among the patriarchs. There is no special priestly caste; there is no temple set aside as the exclusive site of sacrifice. Throughout Genesis, the patriarchs themselves build altars and present offerings at places and times of their own discretion (cf. Gen. 4:3–4; Gen. 8:20–21; Gen. 12:7–8).

At this point in salvation history, family and church are one. Houses are domestic sanctuaries, meals are sacrifices, hearths are altars—all because fathers are empowered as priests by nature.

Still, fathers do not live forever, and so tradition provided a way of preserving family unity when a patriarch died. Upon the death of the patriarch, the family would, ideally, turn to the firstborn son for leadership. The firstborn son serves as a natural mediator between the father and his children. The firstborn is closest to the father; he is in a position of authority among his siblings; and, when the father dies, he is in the best position to assume a paternal, priestly role and preserve the governmental unity of the family. As Rabbi H. C. Brichto has written: "There is ample evidence that the role of priest in the Israelite family had at one time been filled by the firstborn."[1]

In fact, the main plot of the Book of Genesis revolves around the divine blessing that is passed down through the generations, from Adam through Noah to the family of Israel. An important subplot, however, is the patriarchs' struggle to find worthy replacements for firstborns who failed to carry out their responsibilities. Consider how many failed firstborns (e.g., Cain, Ishmael, Esau, Reuben, and Manasseh) are superseded by worthier younger siblings (e.g., Seth, Isaac, Jacob, Joseph, and Ephraim).

Habits of the Hearth

There was a liturgical dimension to the patriarchs' natural priesthood. Saint Jerome, in the fourth century, explained that vestments came with the office. So when Rebekah takes the garments of Esau, her firstborn, and gives them to Jacob (cf. Gen. 27:15), she is symbolically transferring the priestly office. "On this passage," says Jerome, "the Hebrews say that the firstborn discharged the office of priests and had the priestly vestment, clothed in which they offered sacrifices to God, before Aaron was chosen for the priesthood."[2]

---

[1] Rabbi Herbert C. Brichto, "Kin, Cult, Land, and Afterlife—A Biblical Complex," *Hebrew Union College Annual* 44 (1973): 46.

[2] Saint Jerome, *Liber quaestionum hebraicorum in Genesim*, as quoted in *Catholic for a Reason: Scripture and the Mystery of the Family of God* (Steubenville, OH: Emmaus Road, 1998), 223.

We see the same priestly significance, a generation later, in the "long robe" that Jacob gave to his son Joseph (cf. Gen. 37:3–4), and we understand why Joseph's half-brothers were filled with resentment.

Fatherhood, then, is the original basis of priesthood. And the priestly succession of the firstborn is something that follows naturally from the priesthood of the patriarchs. Thus the essential meaning of priesthood goes back to the father in the family—his representative role, spiritual authority and religious service. The firstborn is the father's heir apparent; the one groomed to succeed one day to paternal authority and priesthood within the family.

From the beginning, priesthood belonged to fathers and their "blessed" sons. This historical fact is attested also by Saint Thomas Aquinas, who wrote: "The priesthood also existed before the law . . . for that dignity was allotted to the firstborn."[3]

Defrocked

The pattern continues through Genesis and into the Book of Exodus. There, God declared to Moses at the burning bush, "Israel is my firstborn son" (Ex. 4:22)—that is, Israel was God's heir and His priest. At the Passover, the nation's firstborn sons were redeemed by the blood of the Paschal lamb, and so they were consecrated to serve as priests within each of the twelve tribes and families of Israel (Ex. 19:22–24).

[3] *The Summa Theologica of Saint Thomas Aquinas*, II-II, 87, 1 *ad* 3; in 5 vols., trans. Fathers of the English Dominican Province (Westminster, MD: Christian Classics, 1981), also available from http://www.newadvent.org.

God gave Israel a unique vocation to be a "holy nation and a royal priesthood" (Ex. 19: 5)—an "elder brother" in the family of nations. As the firstborn sons were to be priests in the family, so Israel was to act as God's firstborn son among the nations.

But there was a catch. Israel's status depended upon the biggest "if" in history: "[I]f you obey my voice and keep my covenant" (Ex. 19:5–6).

In this, Israel failed. When the people worshipped the golden calf, the twelve tribes of Israel forfeited the blessing of priesthood to one tribe, the Levites (Ex. 32:25–29). For only the Levites resisted the practice of idolatry, and only the Levites answered Moses' call to avenge the offense by slaughtering the idolaters.

The Levites would, eventually, officiate in Israel's tabernacle. Israel's priesthood thus became a hereditary office reserved to a cultural elite, and the home was no longer the primary place of priesthood and sacrifice. God had essentially "defrocked" the other tribes because of their infidelity. The Levites alone retained exclusive hold on Israel's priesthood through all the succeeding centuries, until the time of Jesus.

The Setting Son

Even so, we can see in the Book of Judges that Israel still identified priesthood with fatherhood. In the seventeenth chapter, we learn of a man named Micah, who consecrates his son a priest for the purpose of worship in the family's domestic shrine.

Yet, when a Levite appears at Micah's door, Micah pleads, "Stay with me, and be to me a father and a priest"

(Judg. 17:10). A chapter later, Micah's plea is echoed, almost verbatim, by the Danites as they invite the Levite to be priest for their entire tribe: "Come with us, and be to us a father and a priest" (Judg. 18:19).

What's most remarkable about those requests is not what they assert, but what they assume. In just a few words, Micah provides us a rare glimpse of a transitional period for the people of Israel. Fathers were still installing their sons as priests in the domestic sanctuary—a custom left over from an earlier age. Yet the Levite's priesthood was already preferred to that of Micah's son—a hint of the newly emerging sacred order.

In this statement of Micah, and its repetition by the Danites, we also see that fatherhood was still considered an essential attribute of priestly ministry—even after priesthood had passed out of the family structure.

These snippets from the Book of Judges are revealing. How embedded in the history of our religion—going back to its Israelite roots—is this overarching reality of the spiritual paternity of the priest (and the priestly role of every father)!

The connection is clear to those who read the Bible carefully. Pope John Paul II has cited those very passages in talking about fatherhood and priesthood: "Israel could also see God as a father by analogy with other figures who had a public and especially religious function and were considered fathers, such as priests."[4]

Israel's sin in the desert was not the final word in salvation history. Nor is it the last word about priesthood and

---

[4] Pope John Paul II, General Audience (January 20, 1999), no. 12.

fatherhood. The *Catechism of the Catholic Church* teaches us that "Everything that the priesthood of the Old Covenant prefigured finds its fulfillment in Christ Jesus, the 'one mediator between God and men' [1 Tim. 2:5]" (no. 1544).

"The Assembly of the Firstborn"

In the fullness of time, God the Father sent Jesus as a faithful firstborn son (cf. Heb. 1:6) and a priest (cf. Heb. 10:21)—not only to restore the natural priesthood, but also to establish a supernatural priesthood within the divine family, the Church.

Thus, with Jesus came a restoration of the natural priesthood of fathers and the establishment of the fatherly order of New Covenant priests. According to the Epistle to the Hebrews, Jesus' role and identity as the faithful firstborn Son of God (cf. Heb 1:6) qualify Him as the perfect mediator between God, His Father, and us, His brothers and sisters. To Christ, we are "the children God has given"(Heb. 2:13), the "many sons" (Heb. 2:10), His "brethren" (Heb. 2:12), the new "descendants of Abraham"(Heb. 2:16), who together form God's "family/household," which Jesus builds and rules as a son (Heb. 3: 3–6). And, as all Christians are identified with Christ, the Church becomes the "assembly of the firstborn" (Heb. 12:23).

Saint Peter, speaking to the Church, takes up the standard that Israel had lost in the desert: "You are a chosen race, a royal priesthood, a holy nation, God's own people" (1 Pet. 2:9).

Now, once again, the home is a sanctuary—Vatican II calls it the "domestic Church." Now, once again, as in the beginning, fathers are priests.

And priests, moreover, are fathers in the Church, which has now become the universal family of God (cf. *Catechism*, nos. 1, 1655). The apostles, who were Christ's first priests, clearly saw their own role as paternal. Saint Paul asserts his spiritual fatherhood: "For though you have countless guides in Christ, you do not have many fathers. For I became your father in Christ Jesus through the gospel" (1 Cor. 4:15; see also Phil. 2:22; 1 Tim. 1:2, 1:18; 2 Tim. 1:2; Tit. 1:4; Philem. 10). Paul was a father not because he was married and reared a family; he did not. He was a father because he was a priest: "a minister . . . in the priestly service of the gospel" (Rom. 15:16).

Saint Augustine, a bishop living just four centuries later, looked upon the episcopal office he had inherited from the apostles in the same way: "The Apostles were sent as fathers; to replace those apostles, sons were born to you who were constituted bishops. . . . The Church calls them fathers, she who gave birth to them, who placed them in the sees of their fathers. . . . Such is the Catholic Church. She has given birth to sons who, through all the earth, continue the work of her first Fathers."[5]

Your Office Is "Calling"

What difference should all this make to the average dad or average priest? It should make all the difference in the world—because, now, fatherhood is not so much a role to be played, as a sacred office, held for life.

---

[5] Saint Augustine, *Psalm 44, 32*, as quoted in Henri De Lubac, *The Motherhood of the Church* (San Francisco: Ignatius Press, 1982), 90.

"For every high priest chosen from among men is appointed to act on behalf of men in relation to God" (Heb. 5:1). In my family, then, I serve as a mediator between God and man, in imitation of Jesus Christ. Before God, I must represent my family and intercede for them. Among my family, I must strive to live as an image of God the Father; for when my children pray to the Father, they will know His fatherhood overwhelmingly through the "revelation" of my example. Priesthood is not something incidental to my fatherhood; it's essential.

To exercise my common priesthood, I must work to make my home a sanctuary and every meal a sacrifice offered to God. In the Hahn household, all of our prayers, works, joys, and sufferings must rise to heaven like incense; every day they're offered heavenward by the man who holds the authority to make that offering. At least one of my children is too small to do so for himself; the others are sometimes too distracted by childhood. The offering of all our lives is a duty that falls to me. This is a responsibility I must assume each day—as mediator, as priest, as father.

Collar I.D.

If we fathers honor our own priesthood, how much more will we honor the priesthood of our pastors, who are configured to Christ in a unique and powerful way. Our priests are more than liturgical professionals—they are fathers. The sacramental priesthood is not so much a ceremonial function as it is a family relation.

Pope John Paul II writes: "[T]he great family which is the Church . . . finds concrete expression in the diocesan and the parish family. . . . No one is without a family in this world: the Church is a home and family for everyone" (*FC*, 85). Our priests are fathers to that "great family"— what an overwhelming task!

What is true of my fatherhood must be much more true in the life of an ordained priest. He is father to a large family. Before God, he must take responsibility for thousands of people. He must represent hundreds of households. He must make an offering of many hidden lives. And his fatherhood is not merely metaphorical. As far back as Aristotle, philosophers have always understood fatherhood as a communication of life. If this is true of natural fatherhood, it is more true of a priest's supernatural fatherhood. As a natural father, I have communicated biological human life—but, in the sacraments of Baptism and the Eucharist, a priest communicates the *divine life* and the *divine humanity* of Jesus Christ.

Because of his spiritual fatherhood, an ordained priest requires our respect—and I mean *every* priest, in spite of his weaknesses, flaws or sins. When God said, "Honor your father and your mother," He didn't qualify the commandment. He gave no exceptions. He never said that, given the following conditions, we could withhold our honor and reverence for a father. This is true in spades regarding the way we honor our priests.

We must honor our fathers in the priesthood, as we honor the priesthood in our fathers. When a man fails either role—in fatherhood or in priesthood—we should pray for him, fast for him, confront him privately with our concerns, confront him with other witnesses; and, if all other attempts fail, we should take our case to the Church, all the while honoring the man, his priesthood, and his fatherhood. This is what children do for their fathers (cf. Gen. 9:22–27).

We should honor our fathers. We should honor our priests. When we do either, we recognize a profound truth about God's family: that fatherhood is a priesthood and that priesthood is a fatherhood.

When we recognize that truth, we honor God, "from whom all fatherhood in heaven and on earth receives its name" (Eph. 3:15).

Postscript

All of these considerations should make it clear why the Church may ordain only men to the priesthood—because nature ordains only men to be fathers. Priesthood is something inscribed by nature, and nature itself is sacramental, a reflection of the supernatural order.

The natural family is a reality that has been created by God. The roles of family members are not interchangeable. Though social engineers have set out to abolish this natural order, their experiments have, without exception, ended by making a stronger case for nature. Men are natural fathers; women are natural mothers. Though I sometimes must stand in for my wife, Kimberly, I can never *be* a mother to my children. And no biotechnological breakthrough can ever make me one. Motherhood has a specific dignity that will always be inaccessible to me, simply because God has created me a man.

As the Old Covenant is ordered to the New, so nature is ordered to grace. Grace does not abolish nature, but builds upon it, completes it and elevates it. So, what is true in the natural order is *perfectly* true in the supernatural.

The natural order of the family is a prototype of the supernatural order of God's family in the Church. In both, the relationships of men and women are not interchangeable. Because a priest is a spiritual father, the Church may bestow Holy Orders only on males. Only males, after all, can be fathers. The ordination of women is impossible, then—as impossible as my becoming a mother.

Chapter Eight

Indecent Exposure
The Unadulterated Truth about Mercy and Judgment

The Gospel story of the adulteress has long been the battleground of scholars who debate big questions about law and the administration of justice. But it's even bigger than that; for it also affects our everyday lives. Must we, for example, remain silent about a friend or family member's sexual immorality? Are we permitted to pass judgment on a public official's character when he's caught in adultery?

The misuse of this story has served to render too many Christians morally mute and reluctant to pass judgment on acts of betrayal. But to reduce the story of the adulteress to a mere "judgment on judgmentalism" is to miss the point entirely.

The story is about a *foolproof* trap laid by the Pharisees to destroy Jesus. In the end, the trap becomes a judgment on the very men who set it.

This Is a Test

The story turns dramatically on a "test" the Pharisees put before Jesus. "Teacher," they said, "this woman has been caught in the act of adultery. Now in the law Moses commanded us to stone such. What do you say about her?" (Jn. 8:4–5).

"What do *You* say about her?" It's a disingenuous question. The Pharisees don't really want Jesus' theological advice; they want His hide. The author of the passage makes that clear: "This they said to test him, that they might have some charge to bring against him" (Jn. 8:6).

And their trap is diabolically ingenious, leaving no way out. The Pharisees framed the question in order to make Jesus choose between the Law of Moses on the one hand, and Roman law on the other. For, though Moses prescribed capital punishment for adulterers, the Romans forbade their subjects to impose the death penalty. Thus, if Jesus answered that the woman should be stoned, He was a dead man—the Pharisees could denounce Him, then, as a dissident before the Roman authorities. Yet, if Jesus answered that the woman should *not* be stoned, He would be thoroughly discredited before the people. What good, after all, is a rabbi who rejects the Law of Moses?

The Pharisees appear to be in a win-win situation. They would have preferred Jesus' death, but they would settle for His professional ruin. So they set their trap. "This they said to test Him."

Yet we've seen Jesus elude such traps before. Consider Matthew 22:15–22, where the Pharisees ask Him about paying taxes to Caesar; Matthew tells us they tried this, unsuccessfully, "to entangle Him." Or, consider Matthew 19:3–9, where the Pharisees "tested Him" by asking whether it is lawful to divorce. In each of these cases, the test is a trap—which in each case springs shut on the Pharisees—but nowhere is the trap so seemingly airtight as in John 8.

Overturning the Tables

Still, Jesus emerges from this test unscathed—and even stronger—merely because He had said, "Let him who is without sin among you be the first to throw a stone at her" (Jn. 8:7). What happened here? What did He mean? Was He indeed overturning Moses' Law?

That was the position of the Protestant reformer Martin Luther. He believed that Jesus was making a clean break from Moses' Law. For "in Christ's realm no punishment is to be found, but only mercy and forgiveness of sins, whereas in the realm of Moses and the world there is no forgiveness of sins, but only wrath and punishment."[1]

Luther saw Christ's righteousness as radically opposed to Moses'. But does this hold water? Did Jesus really come to overturn the Law of Moses? The overwhelming witness of the New Testament indicates otherwise. For Jesus Himself said that He had come not to abolish the Law, but to fulfill it (cf. Mt. 5:17). Elsewhere (cf. Mt. 15:4), He cites—*as normative and binding*—both moral commandments ("Honor your father and your mother") and judicial precepts ("He who speaks evil of father or mother, let him surely die"). And in the passage immediately preceding the story of the adulteress, Jesus rebukes His opponents for not keeping the Law (cf. Jn. 7:19).

Clearly, Jesus would not have set Himself in opposition to the Mosaic Law. In any event, if He had merely rejected Moses, the Pharisees would have scored a minor

---

[1] Martin Luther, *Luther's Works*, ed. Jaroslav Pelikan (Saint Louis: Concilium, 1959), 23.

victory. They could then demonstrate to the people that Jesus was a false prophet; for the Mosaic Law was the standard by which prophets were measured. Yet the Pharisees did not denounce Him, and they did not walk away victorious.

No, neither here, nor anywhere else, did Jesus reject the Mosaic Law.

A Bitter Pill

But what about Roman law? That's where the Pharisees placed their greater hope; for the Romans, not the Pharisees, had the power to kill Jesus (cf. Jn. 18:31).

The Roman occupation of Judea was still a fairly new situation—less than a century old. The Jews chafed at the imposition of Roman law; for, in Israel, there had been no separation of temple and state. The Torah had embodied both the sacred and the secular law. Thus, it was practically impossible for a rabbi to speak on spiritual matters without at least touching on political matters.

Yet such a situation was untenable under the Romans, who would acknowledge no law but their own—but who were incompetent, as non-Jews, to judge according to the Law of Moses.

This situation was a bitter pill for the scribes and Pharisees, who, under self-rule, would have had far greater power and prestige. Under Rome, they were forced to operate in a limited sphere, deciding mostly on questions concerning religious ritual, while referring all civil cases to the Roman authorities. It was a humiliating situation; it compromised the Pharisees, and it diminished their esteem among the people.

Many scholars believe that, during Jesus' lifetime, the Pharisees pursued a campaign to win over the most popular rabbis, so that they could regain the support of the people. Jesus was certainly such a rabbi, drawing crowds of thousands, holding them spellbound, and inspiring men to give up their livelihood in order to follow Him. The scribes and Pharisees must have seen Jesus as just the kind of support they needed. At the start, they must have wanted Him as an ally, believing that with Him on their side, Jewish self-government would be inevitable.

Instead, Jesus gave them His unvarnished contempt, as well as the brunt of His moral and spiritual indictments (cf. Mt. 23:13–33; Mk. 2:17; Lk. 10:46, 11:40–43, 12:1). In their already humiliated condition, this added insult to the Pharisees' injury. So they began to plot His downfall (cf. Mk. 3:6), while they continued to instruct their fellow Jews in the ways of self-righteousness (cf. Mk. 7:1–13).

Still, they remained compromised in the eyes of the people. Moreover, they knew that deliverance unto foreign powers was a curse from Yahweh, a punishment for the sins of Israel. The Pharisees knew the Law well enough to remember that the divine curse was promised to fall upon disobedient and faithless Israel so that she would be overrun by her enemies, who would then impose their ungodly rule upon her (cf. Lev. 26:17, Deut. 4:26–27, 28:32–68).

This is perhaps why the Pharisees took it upon themselves to seek the exact righteousness of the Law—and why the Pharisees felt such resentment and bitterness toward Jesus. The Romans had shamed them with a foreign code of conduct, and then Jesus proceeded to condemn them by their own code! Jesus accused them of breaking the little bit of the Law that the Romans permitted them to follow.

The Showdown

It all begins to sound political. Yet there is a serious spiritual issue at the heart of Jesus' showdown with the Pharisees. Their most fundamental disagreement is over the Pharisees' own standing before God and His Law.

How did the Pharisees see themselves? Consider Saint Paul's testimony about his own standing as a Pharisee. He says that he was "as to the law, a Pharisee . . . as to righteousness under the law blameless" (Phil. 3:5–6). The word "pharisee" itself comes from *parushim*, Hebrew for "separated ones." The Pharisees defined holiness as separation from impurity and defilement. That's why they prided themselves on their superiority to the rabble (cf. Lk. 18:11).

Yet most of the Pharisees we meet in the Gospel are envious of Roman power and of the power and influence of Jesus. It is their self-righteousness that seems most to provoke the anger of Jesus.

In John's Gospel, Jesus' struggle with the Pharisees is depicted as an intense conflict between the forces of light and darkness. This begins early on, in the third chapter, when "a man of the Pharisees named Nicodemus . . . came to Jesus by night" (Jn. 3:1–2). John then proceeds to develop the relationship between Jesus and the Pharisees in terms of cosmic judgment (cf. 3:18–20, 26; 5:22–30). He later says to them: "It is Moses who accuses you, on whom you set your hope. If you believed Moses, you would believe me" (Jn. 5:45–46). Again, when Jesus is teaching in the Temple, He asks them, "Did not Moses give you the law? Yet none of you keeps the law. Why do you seek to kill me?" (Jn. 7:19).

Long before then, however, the Jews had begun to look for an opportunity to kill Jesus, because they perceived Him "making himself equal with God" (Jn. 5:18). Thus, when it was time to go up to Jerusalem for the Feast of Tabernacles, Jesus had to delay His journey and go up privately "because the Jews sought to kill him" (Jn. 7:1). After arriving in secret, Jesus began teaching in the Temple, where He charged the Jews, "Do not judge by appearances, but judge with right judgment" (Jn. 7:24). Even the officers who were sent by Pharisees to arrest Him were so impressed that they returned saying, "No man ever spoke like this man" (Jn. 7:46).

By the end of the seventh chapter, the Pharisees are desperately agitated. Jesus had just finished telling them that the Law that they prided themselves on knowing, they disobeyed. Now it was their turn to challenge Jesus to exercise "right judgment," in a case where "right judgment" could prove disastrous.

Damned If You Do, Damned If You Don't

So the Pharisees set the trap and asked their question, leaving no escape. If Jesus answers one way, He is ripe for execution by the Romans. If He answers another way, He is discredited before the people. If He advises them to stone the woman, He's a dead man. If He advises them to ignore the Law of Moses, He's a has-been and a hypocrite.

So which would it be: hypocrisy or sedition?

Neither. Jesus saw their trap, and He rose above it. He refused to answer yes or no. Perfectly nonchalant, imperturbable, He sat tracing with His finger upon the ground. After a few tense moments, He looked up and uttered His famous line: "Let him who is without sin among you be the first to throw a stone at her" (Jn. 8:7).

And they all walked away.

What happened? Some commentators say that Jesus was simply asking for honest or credible witnesses. But that interpretation encounters two problems. First, what if such a witness had stepped forward? If Jesus had authorized such a witness to stone her, He would also have been authorizing His own death sentence from Rome. The second problem is that such an interpretation would imply that on this one single occasion, Jesus pricked the conscience of the Pharisees, *each and every Pharisee*—in public, before onlookers. But there's absolutely no evidence to support such a reading. Neither before nor after this incident do the Pharisees show any openness to repent in response to Jesus. In the end, they will be among His false accusers before Pontius Pilate.

So, then . . . did Jesus really convince the Pharisees that no one on earth was capable of judging? Is this the end of "judgmentalism"?

Their Plan Backfires

No. Jesus foiled their plan. He knew the situation. He knew that the woman stood condemned before God's Law. But He also knew that God's Law had no civil force within Israel at the moment. Moreover, He knew the spiritual self-understanding of the Pharisees. So He countered their challenge with a far more ingenious one of His own: "Let him who is without sin among you be the first to throw a stone at her."

At first, to the Pharisees, this probably sounded like an invitation to proceed—and thus a fatal blunder on Jesus' part. "'Him who is without sin'—hey, that sounds like us!" Remember, the Pharisees thought of themselves as sinless and righteous, and everybody knew it. But the Pharisees also knew that Jesus disagreed. He had condemned them as the vilest sinners in all Judea, and surely there were many among the crowd who were only too eager to agree with Jesus.

Now the tables were turned, and *the Pharisees* had to choose! If they stoned her, they would bring the wrath of Rome upon *themselves;* and *they* would surely die for the crime of sedition. But, if they did *not* stone her, they would expose their own claims of righteousness as utterly false.

Suddenly, the Pharisees were faced with the very choice they had tried to force upon Jesus: to die or be discredited.

Balanced Judgment

Their public reputation for sinlessness was apparently not worth their lives. They walked away, beginning with the oldest, for the older men were more politically astute.

Meanwhile, our Savior looked on. He was vindicated; they were convicted; and He had accomplished all this without compromising a jot or tittle of the sacred Law of God as it was revealed to Moses.

The Pharisees knew the Law. Ignorance was not their problem. Pride was their problem. They wanted to hold the prestigious authority of the Law while retaining their own self-righteousness. Christ dared to call them on their sin and hypocrisy. And when they were confronted with true right-eousness in Jesus Christ, they were threatened and exposed. "When they heard it, they went away" (Jn. 8:9).

But what about the woman caught in adultery? Notice that Jesus did not condemn her, but neither did He apologize for her public shame. He does not refrain from judgment. Judgment, after all, is a precondition of mercy. Jesus sets her free, but He makes clear that mercy has its price, and that price is the fulfillment of the Law: "Go, and do not sin again" (Jn. 8:11).

Postscript: Canon Fodder

The misuse of this passage is not something new. In fact, the story is actually missing from many ancient manuscripts of John's Gospel, and many modern versions of the Bible relegate it to a footnote or place it in brackets. (Indeed, some of the ancient manuscripts that omit the story do so with an indication that "something has been left out." This is otherwise unprecedented in the New Testament.)

Apparently, in the early Church, the passage was some-times omitted in order to avoid scandal. Saint Augustine explained that moral rigorists tended to exclude the story because they feared it could lead people to a lax attitude about adultery.

At the Council of Trent, when the biblical canon was defined, this passage was authoritatively included in the Vulgate. The Magisterium confirmed the story's place in the New Testament more than once in the twentieth century.

Chapter Nine

The Hour Is Coming
How Should We Read the Signs of the Times?

What's in an hour? Modern physicists tell us in theory what cave dwellers surely knew from experience: that time is elastic. An hour sometimes passes too quickly, as when the conversation is sublime or the company sweet. An hour can also seem endless, as I learned one winter, when I continued to lecture during a severe bout with the flu.

Jesus, being God, could pack an eternity of goodness into an hour. Indeed, from the beginning of His ministry, He seems to have kept a singular focus on His "hour." In this chapter, we're going to study Jesus' frequent use of the word "hour"—especially in the Gospel according to John.

Arresting Ideas

Throughout the pages of John's Gospel, Jesus refers to the moment when His mission would be fulfilled as His "hour." The word "hour"—in Greek, *hora*—has a specific literal sense in the Gospel. For John and for Jesus, the word denotes the culminating moment of Jesus' life and mission, the historical events of His sacrificial self-offering. "So they sought to arrest him; but no one laid hands on him, because *his hour* had not yet come" (Jn. 7:30). And again: "[H]e taught in the temple; but no one arrested him, because *his hour* had not yet come" (Jn. 8:20).

The references to Jesus' arrest make it obvious when His "hour" would come. It would come in the final days of His earthly life, with His suffering, death, and Resurrection. But it would involve much more. When we look at the Fourth Gospel in its entirety, and search out all the references to Jesus' "hour," we find a deeper *spiritual sense* to the word. Taken together, all the "hours" of John's Gospel point to a time that began so many centuries ago in a city in Palestine; but they point also, quite clearly and specifically, to a time and a place that you and I know with easy familiarity.

This chapter, then, will be an exercise in "spiritual exegesis." Together, we'll search out the mystical, allegorical, and prophetic ways that Jesus used the word "hour." For He could have chosen another word. In Aramaic and Greek, as in modern English, options abound. Jesus could have spoken of His "moment," His "day," or His "time." Yet He chose "hour," and He used it in a way that is remarkably consistent—and with a powerful cumulative effect.

This is spiritual exegesis. I must emphasize, however, that the "spiritual sense" of the Bible does not originate in the imagination of the reader, but in the mind of God. In other words, I'm not making this up; I'm searching it out. Spiritual exegesis must never contradict the literal sense of Scripture—which is always the primary sense—and it must always square with the Church's teaching and Tradition.

No Wine before It's Time

Jesus used the word "hour" to speak about the central mystery of faith, the work He had come to accomplish. His first recorded use of the word is on the day of His first recorded miracle, the wedding feast at Cana in Galilee. He arrives at the feast that Sunday along with His mother and His disciples. Soon afterward, the party runs out of wine—an embarrassing situation for the newlyweds—and Mary says to her Son, "They have no wine." Jesus replies: "O woman, what have you to do with me? *My hour* has not yet come" (Jn. 2:3–4).

Does His response strike you as odd? Mary had made a simple, empirical observation—the wine had run out. But Jesus appears to read far too much into it. His response— "O woman, what have you to do with me? My hour has not yet come"—seems way out of proportion to Mary's simple report. But maybe not.

To make sense of Jesus' assertion, "My hour has not yet come," we must identify the underlying assumption. Clearly, He anticipates an "hour" when something momentous will happen. Yet that time is not now. We can compare it to an engaged man inviting his fiancée to his bedroom to see his etchings. The fiancée would be right to respond: "What are you saying? Our hour has not yet come." Again, the assumption is that the hour will one day come—when it will be proper for them to enter his bedroom—but not yet.

But what was the assumption underlying the conversation at Cana? What could possibly have reminded Jesus of His "hour"? What in His mother's request even remotely suggests the still-distant time of Jesus' self-offering? Let's look at the rest of the scene, to see if we can search out some detail that the wedding feast had in common with the hour of Jesus' Passion, death, and Resurrection.

Mary's request had an amazing effect on her Son. "Now six stone jars were standing there . . . each holding twenty or thirty gallons. Jesus said to them, 'Fill the jars with water.' And they filled them up to the brim. He said to them, 'Now draw some out, and take it to the steward of the feast.' . . . When the steward of the feast tasted the water now become wine, . . . [he] called the bridegroom and said to him, 'Every man serves the good wine first; and when men have drunk freely, then the poor wine; but you have kept the good wine until now'" (Jn. 2:6–10).

What does this story tell us about Jesus' hour? Cana, we are told, was the first of Jesus' "signs." John uses the word "sign" instead of "wonder" or "miracle," because he wishes to highlight the symbolic meaning behind the miracles. A sign is a miracle, yes, but also a harbinger of something greater.

Look back through the exchange between Jesus and His mother. Only one thing in Mary's request could have triggered such a response: "They have no wine."

Jesus knew that when His hour did arrive, He would provide wine—indeed, the finest of wine. But that definitive hour had not yet come.

Worship in Spirit and Truth

Let's move on to the next instance of the "hour." In the fourth chapter, Jesus is speaking with a person who today might be called "marginalized." She was a Samaritan, a member of a rebel people who, though they were descended from Israel, had for centuries observed a degraded and idolatrous religion. Devout Jews did not stoop to speak with Samaritans. Yet Jesus chose this Samaritan woman to receive the first explicit teaching about His "hour." After she speaks of the religious differences between Jews and

Samaritans, He replies: "Woman, believe me, *the hour* is coming when neither on this mountain nor in Jerusalem will you worship the Father. . . . [T]he *hour* is coming, and now is, when the true worshipers will worship the Father in spirit and truth" (Jn. 4:21–24).

Once more, we find Him speaking of His hour, but again it goes beyond the historical events surrounding His passion. At Cana, His words revealed that He expected to provide wine when the hour came. Now, with the Samaritan woman, He reveals another dimension.

In this passage, we learn that His hour is not only a time of providing wine. It is even more a time of worship—a radically new way of worship, which even the Jews in the Jerusalem Temple had never known. When the hour comes, the living water of the Holy Spirit will be poured out to enable all people to worship "in spirit."

That outpouring changed everything. Now, in Jesus' hour, it's not *where* you worship that's important, but *how* you worship. Nor is worship restricted to the Chosen People or the Jerusalem Temple. Worship "in spirit" is available even to those people whom the Jews had considered "spiritually dead." But how can this be? The answer, again, is in the hour.

Hour of the Living Dead

Jesus returned to the theme of His hour in John 5:25, as He explained why He was healing on the Sabbath. He told the crowd: "Truly, truly, I say to you, *the hour* is coming, and now is, when the dead will hear the voice of the Son of God, and those who hear will live" (Jn. 5:25–29).

Here is a third dimension of the hour. Not only is it a time of worship when the "best wine" will be provided, it is also a time when the Word of God will bring people to repentance and forgiveness—in short, to new life.

Greeks Bearing Gifts

Jesus' next discussion of His hour takes place at Passover (cf. Jn. 12:20–23). In Jerusalem, some Greeks approach Philip and request an audience with Jesus. Philip and Andrew inform Jesus, perhaps expecting Him to say, "Send them in." But, as at Cana, Jesus responds in a way that is unexpected, even bewildering. He replies: "The hour has come for the Son of man to be glorified. Truly, truly, I say to you, unless a grain of wheat falls into the earth and dies, it remains alone; but if it dies, it bears much fruit" (Jn. 12:23–24).

Wait a minute. The apostles tell Jesus that some Greeks are here to see Him, and He responds by saying His hour had come, and by speaking of death and fruit and grains of wheat? This surely must make sense—but how? The apostles must have been baffled. They had made a simple request, and, in response, Jesus preached a sermon. We never even find out whether Jesus met with the Greeks!

There's a lot going on in this rich passage. Let's examine the details, one by one.

Against the Grain

First, you'll notice that the exchange took place at Passover, the Jewish feast commemorating Israel's liberation from slavery in Egypt. The central rite of the Passover feast was the sacrifice of a spotless lamb. In John's Gospel,

Jesus is explicitly called the "Lamb of God" (1:29, 36). The "hour" of the Lamb, then, is Passover. This Passover is more significant because, now, not just the children of Israel, but the nations—the Gentiles, the Greeks—have come to find liberation.

So now would be a good time for Jesus to use the "Lamb" metaphor, right? But He doesn't. He speaks of wheat instead, and He speaks of wheat "dying" to produce "much fruit." And how would that fruit manifest itself, once the grains were harvested? As bread, of course.

Now is *the hour*, Jesus says. It is Passover. Jesus is the Lamb. And He is speaking of His own sacrifice. It becomes even more explicit in later verses, when, speaking again of His hour, He says, "Now is my soul troubled. And what shall I say? 'Father, save me from this *hour?*' No, for this purpose I have come to this *hour*. Father, glorify thy name" (Jn. 12:27–28).

We must not miss the importance of this moment in the divine drama. Jesus is offering Himself here as the perfect sacrifice. We must be clear about this: He was *offering* Himself. Jesus was not the hapless victim of a Roman execution; He was a victim of love. His life was not taken; it was given (cf. Jn. 10:17–18). Before Pilate, Caiphas, or Herod could decree His death, Jesus gave up His life. Before anyone could lay a hand on Him, He celebrated the Passover, and He transformed the Passover into the Holy Eucharist—the fruit of the grain of wheat, after it has fallen into the ground and died.

All this was, John tells us, "before the feast of the Passover, when Jesus knew that *his hour* had come to depart out of this world to the Father" (Jn. 13:1). Just a few days later, we know from the other three Gospels, Jesus blessed the bread and the chalice of wine, pronouncing them to be His Body and Blood. Curiously, John's is the only Gospel that does not recount those particular details of the Passover meal. Yet John does tell us more about the rest of that supper. Toward the end of the meal, John relates, Jesus "lifted up his eyes to heaven and said, 'Father, *the hour* has come; glorify thy Son that the Son may glorify thee, since thou hast given him power over all flesh, to give eternal life to all whom thou hast given him.'" (Jn. 17:1–2).

We know when this will happen: the hour. We know what will happen: human beings will participate in the glory and communion shared by the Father and the Son—"in the Spirit." In the passage that tradition calls His "high-priestly prayer," Jesus prays: "that they may all be one; even as thou, Father, art in me, and I in thee, that they also may be [one] in us" (Jn. 17:21). Don't miss the significance of what Jesus' hour will bring. Jesus is not saying that our oneness will be *like* the oneness of the Trinity; He's saying our oneness will *be* the oneness of the Trinity—not something similar, but identical! In that hour, we will "come to share in the divinity of Christ, who humbled himself to share in our humanity."[1] In that hour, we will know the most intimate communion with God.

---

[1] "Order of Mass with a Congregation," in *The Sacramentary: Approved for Use in the Dioceses of the United States of America by the National Conference of Catholic Bishops and Confirmed by the Apostolic See,* trans. International Commission on English in the Liturgy (New York: Catholic Book Publishing, 1985), 370.

And, immediately after uttering this prayer, Jesus was arrested and carried off to be executed. With this event, began the most literal, historical meaning of "the hour."

To the Point
Besides the obvious literal meaning—the historical event of the Cross—what else have we learned about Jesus' understanding of the hour? In the hour:

—We receive wine, the best wine (cf. Jn. 2:1–11).
—We are empowered to worship in a new way: in spirit and truth (cf. Jn. 4:23–24).
—We hear God's Word in order to receive new life (cf. Jn. 5:25).
—We gather together as "Greeks" and "Jews" to celebrate the new Passover (cf. Jn. 4:23, 12:20, 13:1).
—We receive the living bread, the fruit borne of the grain of wheat that has died (cf. Jn. 12:23–24).
—We will see the Lamb of God lifted up, drawing all men to Himself (cf. Jn. 12:32).

Take a second look at that list: bread and wine, the Word of the Lord, spiritual worship, a new Passover for Jews and Greeks. What does this add up to?

It's the Mass! The Mass is the hour when all this takes place—and Jesus knew it from the start. Moreover, He prepared His mother and disciples to grasp the deeper mystery of how His self-offering on the Cross would be re-presented for all time. At Mass, we receive bread of finest wheat, with the best of wine. There, we offer spiritual worship that is open to all people. There, we hear the Word of God and receive forgiveness for our sins—new life amid spiritual death. There, we mark the new Passover and behold the Lamb of God, "who takes away the sins of the world." (And all of this, coincidentally, takes about *an hour* to complete on the average Sunday, at least in my parish!)

Yes, Jesus' death and Resurrection marked His finest hour; but His last Passover meal was not merely a warm-up, or a stop along the way to greater things. Jesus saw it as an essential part of the main event of His life. To Him, it was a part of that definitive moment, His "hour." The Apostle John was careful to show that the Eucharist was an urgent concern of Jesus' own heart, that it held a central place in Jesus' self-awareness and in His awareness of His mission.

The Mass is, in a sense, *the point* of John's Gospel and Jesus' mission. Whenever Jesus focused on His "hour," He saw His death and Resurrection, yes; but He also saw beyond these events to their extension throughout time and space in the celebration of the Eucharistic liturgy. These elements—His suffering, death, Resurrection, and Eucharist—are all of a piece. Together, they are the one Paschal Mystery. In the Old Covenant, *paschal* meant Passover; in the new, it means Easter. In the Eucharist, which is our participation in the Easter mystery, we "pass over" to new life that is eternal (cf. Jn. 17:1–5).

Tough Talk

Throughout his Gospel, then, John makes it clear that the Eucharist is a central mystery of Christ's life. Even apart from our discussion of Jesus' hour, we see that John's Gospel provides further confirmation of the centrality of the Eucharist. The most explicit teaching on Jesus' Real Presence in the sacrament comes in the sixth chapter. There, Jesus Himself declares that He is the "Bread of Life" (6:35, 48). As the Jews "murmur" against this teaching, Jesus states it even more graphically: "I am the living bread which came down from heaven; if any one eats of this bread, he will live for ever; and the bread which I shall give for the life of the world is my flesh" (Jn. 6:51). When the Jews' murmuring grows hostile, He makes Himself perfectly clear: "Truly, truly, I say to you, unless you eat the flesh of the Son of man and drink his blood, you have no life in you; he who eats my flesh and drinks my blood has eternal life, and I will raise him up at the last day. For my flesh is food indeed, and my blood is drink indeed. He who eats my flesh and drinks my blood abides in me, and I in him" (Jn. 6:53–57).

Like all the Paschal Mysteries—like immortal God dying on the Cross, like a man rising from the dead—the mystery of the Real Presence is a "hard saying" (Jn. 6:60), the kind of teaching that makes some disciples turn away in disgust (cf. Jn. 6:66). Yet it is something that all the other Gospels and Saint Paul attest as well (cf. Mt. 26:26–28, Mk. 14:22–25, Lk. 22:19–20; 1 Cor. 11:23–26). If the words "this is my body . . . this is my blood" (Mt. 26:28) are not plain enough, we have the Gospel of John to make matters perfectly clear: The Eucharist is Jesus' Body, Blood, soul, and divinity. In other words, the Eucharist is our experience, right now, of the life we'll know in eternity. It is our participation in the life of the Trinity, our identification with Jesus in His eternal self-offering to the Father. Put simply: The Mass is heaven on earth.

What's at Stake

What practical difference does all this make? If, as Christians, we are to imitate Jesus Christ, we must make the Eucharist as central to our lives as it was to His. We must make it our own "hour," for which we long and toward which we journey. How do we do this?

The eleventh chapter of Saint Paul's First Letter to the Corinthians is a veritable handbook for living the liturgy well. We should be reverent at Mass, and dress properly; we should put away our grudges beforehand; we should take the Host and the chalice with decorum; we should examine our conscience and do penance. Above all, we should *believe* in the Eucharist as Jesus teaches us to believe, knowing in our hearts that this Mass—and specifically, your Communion and my Communion—is the reason God became a man, and suffered, and died, and rose again. This is serious business. Saint Paul says: "Whoever, therefore, eats the bread or drinks the cup of the Lord in an unworthy manner will be guilty of profaning the body and blood of the Lord. . . . For any one who eats and drinks without discerning the body, eats and drinks judgment upon himself. That is why many of you are weak and ill, and some have died" (1 Cor. 11: 27, 29–30). Serious business, indeed.

The first Christians took this teaching very seriously. We have the evidence in Saint John's own disciples.

Saint Polycarp, a bishop and martyr of the second century, was a follower of John, having studied under the Apostle as a young boy and then living to a ripe old age. Around the year 155, when Saint Polycarp was in his eighties, he was condemned to be burned at the stake. From the pyre, he prayed in words that read like an

Eucharistic prayer. It is interesting, for example, that John's disciple should speak of martyrdom as his "hour" and his "sacrifice": "I give You thanks that You have counted me worthy of this day and this hour, that I should have a part in the number of Your martyrs . . . among whom may I be accepted this day before You as a rich and acceptable sacrifice, as You, the ever-truthful God, have foreordained."[2]

In his own "hour," as he faced imminent and unimaginable pain, perhaps Saint Polycarp remembered the words of Jesus, which had been recorded by the bishop's own master, John: "Indeed, the *hour* is coming when whoever kills you will think he is offering service to God" (Jn. 16:2). Or maybe he found comfort where Jesus, in the same discourse, again talks about the "hour" of His disciples: "When a woman is in travail she has sorrow, because her *hour* has come; but when she is delivered of the child, she no longer remembers the anguish, for joy that a child is born into the world. So you have sorrow now, but I will see you again and your hearts will rejoice, and no one will take your joy from you" (Jn. 16:21–22).

Martyrs' Meal

According to some traditions, Saint Ignatius of Antioch, yet another early martyr, was also a disciple of John. Such tutelage shows, perhaps, in the Eucharistic imagery of the letters Ignatius wrote as he traveled to Rome, the place of his martyrdom in 107. "I am the wheat of God," he wrote

---

[2] Saint Polycarp, as quoted in *The Martyrdom of Saint Polycarp, Bishop of Smyrna*, no. 14:2, author's translation.

to the Romans, "and am ground by the teeth of the wild beasts, that I may be found the pure bread of God."[3]

The Eucharist is inseparable from Christ's Passion and death and self-offering; and His sacrifice is likewise inseparable from the many small sacrifices of our own lives, if only we desire it. How beautiful it is that some of the early Christians referred to the Mass as "The Lord's Passion." It is no surprise that the Church's most ancient worship also reflects Jesus' powerful teaching about His "hour," which, by then, was understood to be the liturgy itself. The rites attributed to Saint Mark gave thanks to God because He had "brought us unto this hour, permitting us to stand before You in Your holy place."[4] The Liturgy of Saint James, which is probably even more ancient, begs God to "make us, who are unworthy, worthy of this hour."[5]

The spiritual sense of John's Gospel tells the profound truth about the Holy Eucharist, a truth that Jesus states in a more literal fashion in the sixth chapter of the same Gospel. Christ did not leave us, His disciples, unprepared for His sacred mysteries. He has been preparing us for this hour since the moment He began His ministry.

[3] Saint Ignatius of Antioch, chap. IV, in *The Epistle of Ignatius to the Romans*, in *ANF*, vol. 1, eds. Alexander Roberts and James Donaldson (Peabody, MA: Hendrickson, 1994), 75.

[4] *The Divine Liturgy of the Holy Apostle and Evangelist Mark, the Disciple of Holy Peter*, no. I, in *ANF*, vol. 7, eds. Alexander Roberts and James Donaldson (Peabody, MA: Hendrickson, 1994), 551.

[5] *The Divine Liturgy of Saint James, the Holy Apostle and Brother of the Lord*, no. XIX, in *ANF*, vol. 7, 540.

Chapter Ten

Come Again?
The Real Presence as Parousia

There is a world of difference between the way we talk about the Real Presence today and the way the ancient Church talked about the doctrine.

Catholics today often speak of the Real Presence in terms of a crisis—that is, a crisis of faith. In 1992, a Gallup poll concluded that only thirty percent of Catholics in the United States believe that the bread and wine become the Body and Blood of Christ, while "nearly seventy percent . . . hold erroneous beliefs about Christ's presence in the Eucharist."[1] Thus, a large majority would seem to disbelieve, or simply not know, the Church's perennial teaching: "At the heart of the Eucharistic celebration are the bread and wine that, by the word of Christ and the invocation of the Holy Spirit, become Christ's Body and Blood" (*Catechism*, no. 1333).

A 1997 study produced results similar to those of 1994. Since then, bishops, catechists, and even scholars have worried about this data, and pondered how the Church might solve the problem.

---

[1] Rev. Frank Chacon and Jim Burnham, introduction to *Beginning Apologetics 3: How to Explain and Defend the Real Presence of Christ in the Eucharist* (Farmington, NM: San Juan Catholic Seminars, 2000), 4.

The *Catechism of the Catholic Church* provides an excellent beginning, in a section titled "The presence of Christ by the power of his word and the Holy Spirit" (nos. 1373–1381). The section states the fact of the Real Presence and speaks at some length about the process that converts the elements of bread and wine into Christ's Body and Blood. "This change the holy Catholic Church has fittingly and properly called transubstantiation [Council of Trent (1551): DS 1642; cf. Mt. 26:26 ff.; Mk. 14:22 ff.; Lk. 22:19 ff.; 1 Cor. 11:24 ff.]" (no. 1376). The *Catechism* then moves to the logical conclusion of belief in transubstantiation: adoring worship of the Eucharist.

The word *transubstantiation* is fitting and proper, and the *Catechism*'s description of the process is succinct yet profound. But these are not the ultimate solution to the Church's crisis of Eucharistic faith. For the term describes a process, but not the end result of that process. For that, we need to press on in our study and contemplation. As the *Catechism* itself reminds us: "We do not believe in formulas, but in those realities they express, which faith allows us to touch. 'The believer's act of faith does not terminate in the propositions, but in the realities which they express' [Saint Thomas Aquinas, *STh* II-II, 1, 2 *ad* 2]" (no. 170).

What is the reality expressed by the formula? What, in essence, is the presence that faith allows us to touch?

In this study, I would like to return to the sources of Christian doctrine, Scripture and Tradition, to discover—and recover—the authentic understanding of Jesus' Real Presence. Therein, I believe, lies the resolution of the crisis of Eucharistic faith, and many other crises as well, both personal and communal.

Opening Presence

The early Christians also spoke of the Real Presence in terms of crisis, but a different sort of crisis. They spoke of the Real Presence in the language of *apocalypse*—the second coming, the consummation of history, the end of the world. Indeed, in the works of the Church Fathers and in the earliest liturgies, "Eucharist" and "second coming" are often treated as equivalent terms. The Eucharist is the awaited parousia, the coming of Christ, exactly as Jesus Himself promised it would be, exactly as Saint Paul described it, exactly as Saint John saw it "in the Spirit on the Lord's day" (Rev. 1:10).

The Eucharist is the parousia. I have given many lectures on this subject since 1999, when I published *The Lamb's Supper: The Mass as Heaven on Earth*. In that book, I examined the Book of Revelation in light of the liturgies of the Church and of Israel, and I examined the Church's Mass in light of the biblical Apocalypse. Most of my readers and listeners were aware that the Book of Revelation had something to say about the coming of Jesus at the end of the world. Few knew, however, that the Book of Revelation had anything to say about Jesus' coming in the Eucharist.

The idea seems alien to faithful churchgoers in the twenty-first century. Yet it was commonplace to Christians of the first, second, and third centuries; and, to scholars of history—whether Catholic or not—the notion appears so pervasive as to be obvious. The great historical theologian Jaroslav Pelikan, writing as a Lutheran, observed of the early Church: "The coming of Christ was 'already' and 'not yet': he had come already—in the incarnation, and on the basis of the incarnation would come in the Eucharist; he had come already in the Eucharist, and would come at the last in the new cup that he would drink with them in his Father's kingdom."[2]

Though a final parousia will one day come, the Eucharist is the parousia here and now. Anglican scholar Gregory Dix wrote that this notion was "universal" by the third century, and probably long before, since he adds that there are no exceptions to this rule: "[N]o pre-Nicene author Eastern or Western whose Eucharistic doctrine is at all fully stated" holds a different view.[3]

Consider just two examples. The ancient Jerusalem liturgy of Saint James announces: "Let all mortal flesh be silent, and stand with fear and trembling, and meditate nothing earthly within itself: for the King of kings and Lord of lords, Christ our God, comes forward."[4] The Egyptian liturgy of Saint Sarapion proclaims: "This sacrifice is full of your glory."[5] Similar passages can be found in

---

[2] Jaroslav Pelikan, *The Emergence of the Catholic Tradition (100–600)*, vol. 1, in *The Christian Tradition: A History of the Development of Doctrine* series (Chicago: University of Chicago Press, 1971), 126. See also Oscar Cullmann, "The Meaning of the Lord's Supper in Primitive Christianity," in *Essays on the Lord's Supper*, in *Ecumenical Studies in Worship* series, no. 1 (London: Lutterworth, 1958), 15: "Hence, in the early Church, the Lord's Supper involved the presence of Christ in its threefold relation with Easter, with the cult and with the *Parousia*."
[3] Gregory Dix, *The Shape of the Liturgy* (London: A&C Black, 1945), 252–53.
[4] "The Cherubic Hymn," in *The Divine Liturgy of Saint James, the Holy Apostle and Brother of the Lord*, sect. II, in *ANF*, vol. 7, eds. Alexander Roberts and James Donaldson (Peabody, MA: Hendrickson, 1994), 540.
[5] John Wordsworth, ed. and trans., *Bishop Sarapion's Prayer-Book: An Egyptian Summary Dated Probably about A.D. 350–356* (London: Society for Promoting Christian Knowledge, 1899), 61.

the liturgies of Saint Mark, Saint Hippolytus, the Apostolic Constitutions, Saint John Chrysostom, Saint Cyril of Alexandria, as well as the Roman Canon.[6]

What the ancients saw in the liturgy was the coming of Christ, the parousia; and what they meant by parousia is what we today should mean by the Real Presence. But our ancestors seem to have held that belief more firmly, and understood it more fully, than most Catholics do today.

If we want to recover such universality of belief, we might start again at the beginning. Thus, I propose to revisit a number of relevant biblical texts and read them with the Church Fathers, to see what so many people today are missing when they go to Mass.

Get Real

When I say that we speak differently of the Real Presence today, I do not mean to imply that the content of faith has changed. It hasn't. In fact, the *Catechism of the Catholic Church* presents much of its Eucharistic doctrine in quotations from Church Fathers who lived before the year 200. The *Catechism* echoes the flesh-and-blood realism of the earliest Christians when it says: "[T]he bread and wine . . . become Christ's Body and Blood" (no. 1333).

To say this is to take Jesus Christ at His word: "This is my body" (Lk. 22:19), He pronounced over the bread at the Last Supper. And He preached at the synagogue of Capernaum: "I am the living bread which came down from heaven; if any one eats of this bread, he will live for

---

[6] For an excellent discussion of these and similar passages, see Jerome Gassner, O.S.B., *The Canon of the Mass* (New York: Herder, 1950), 158.

ever; and the bread which I shall give for the life of the world is my flesh" (Jn. 6:51).

What did these statements mean to the early Church? In the year 107, Saint Ignatius of Antioch said that it was a mark of true faith to confess the Eucharist "to be the flesh of our Savior Jesus Christ, which suffered for our sins, and which the Father, in His goodness, raised up again."[7] Some fifty years later, Saint Justin Martyr wrote that "the food blessed by the prayer of His word . . . is the flesh and blood of Jesus who was made flesh."[8]

"Bread and wine" become "Body and Blood." The Church took Christ at His word. This doctrine faced no significant challenge in the first Christian millennium. In every generation and in every geographic corner of the Church, the Fathers bore witness to the Real Presence: Irenaeus of Lyons, Hippolytus of Rome, Tertullian of Carthage, Clement of Alexandria, Cyril of Jerusalem, John Chrysostom of Antioch. Even Theodore of Mopsuestia, a man whose christology of "indwelling" was condemned as heretical, could not bring himself to speak of the Eucharist in any but the realistic and sacramental terms of the Church—even though that realism was incompatible with his own theological method.[9]

---

[7] Saint Ignatius of Antioch, *Epistle of Ignatius to the Smyrneans*, chap. VII, in *ANF*, vol. 1, eds. Alexander Roberts and James Donaldson (Peabody, MA: Hendrickson, 1994), 89.

[8] Saint Justin Martyr, *The First Apology of Justin*, as quoted in Mike Aquilina, *The Mass of the Early Christians* (Huntington, IN: Our Sunday Visitor, 2001), 41.

[9] Cf. Pelikan, *The Christian Tradition*, 236–37.

The early Christians spoke with one voice in this matter. Yet they did not speak at length; for they observed a certain discretion, which today we call the "discipline of the secret." The sacraments were most sacred—they were actions of the Lord Himself—and so they were not to be publicly disputed, scientifically probed, or otherwise subjected to unnecessary scrutiny.

Since no one disputed the doctrine, philosophical theology had little to say about the Real Presence until the turn of the second millennium. Only then did heresies arise to challenge the doctrine; only then did theologians develop a technical vocabulary, in order to refute the heresies.

Paul in Person

But it is not the specialized vocabulary that I want to examine here. Those terms are helpful, but they are secondary. In this brief space, I wish instead to look at what is primary.

Thus, it is to the Bible I want to return, to certain inspired words about Jesus' Real Presence.

It is easy enough to see where in Scripture the Fathers learned their flesh-and-blood realism. Christ's Eucharistic words are plain enough, in the sixth chapter of John's Gospel and in the four accounts of the Last Supper (cf. Mt. 26:27–29; Mk. 14:22–25; Lk. 22:14–20; 1 Cor. 11:23–26).

But where in the New Testament did they find their Eucharistic understanding of the parousia—which seems so unlike the modern ideas of both the Real Presence and the second coming.

The Greek word *parousia* means "coming, arrival, or advent." In Christian parlance, it has come to mean, specifically, Christ's return in glory at the end of time. Jesus Himself used the term many times in describing this eschatological event. For example: "as the lightning comes from the east and shines as far as the west, so will be the coming [parousia] of the Son of man" (Mt. 24:27).

Because of such passages, it can be difficult for us to think of parousia as meaning anything but a "coming in glory"—a dramatic divine interruption of history. But that is a theological projection onto a fairly common, and even mundane, Greek word. "Coming in glory" was not the meaning of the word in its original usage. Parousia could describe the visit of an emperor or king, and it was sometimes used that way. It could also describe a much less impressive event. When Saint Paul, for example, speaks of his own parousia, he gives it a decidedly self-deprecating cast: "For they [Paul's critics] say, 'His letters are weighty and strong, but his bodily presence [parousia] is weak, and his speech of no account'" (2 Cor. 10:10).

Note that, here, all Paul means by his own parousia is his "bodily presence," which he insists is unimpressive to the senses. He uses the word in the same sense in his letter to the Philippians: "Therefore, my beloved, as you have always obeyed, so now, not only as in my presence [parousia] but much more in my absence, work out your own salvation with fear and trembling" (Phil. 2:12).

In both passages, Paul uses parousia to mean an immediate bodily presence, a presence that is real, though visually and aurally unimposing.

Is it not likely that Jesus used the word parousia to connote the same things? Is it not possible that He meant a bodily presence that was real, but unimposing to the senses?

I acknowledge that this is not the interpretation of parousia given by many modern preachers, especially among evangelical and fundamentalist Protestants. But consider the expectations of Jesus' own generation. The Jews of His time read the Old Testament prophecies as predictions of a messiah who would come with military power, overwhelming his enemies with spectacular victories. They were not prepared for a carpenter who laid down His life as a victim.

Instant Gratification

Jesus had promised repeatedly that the kingdom was coming without delay. Midway through the "little apocalypse" of Matthew's Gospel, Jesus says: "Truly, I say to you, this generation will not pass away till all these things take place" (Mt. 24:35).

The early Christians expected immediate fulfillment of Jesus' prophecies. They expected an imminent parousia. Modern historians have found evidence of this expectation throughout the New Testament and the earliest Christian writings. The most ancient Eucharistic prayer that has survived, in the *Didache*, ends with the Aramaic word *Maranatha*, that is, "Come, Lord!" The Book of Revelation begins with a promise to show "what must soon take place" (Rev. 1:1) and ends with the same words as the liturgy in the *Didache:* "Come, Lord Jesus!" Biblical scholar Margaret Barker has identified this word—

Maranatha!—as the Church's primal Eucharistic prayer: "This links the return of the LORD to the Eucharist. Other lines of the [*Didache's*] prayer are ambiguous: 'Let this present world pass away', for example, could imply either a literal understanding of the LORD's return or the present transforming effect of the Eucharist. Maranatha in the Eucharist, however, must be the original epiklesis, praying for the coming of the LORD."[10]

Modern historians are right to point out the expectation of the apostolic age. They go wrong, however, when they conclude that the early Christians must have been disappointed with the passing of time. The apostate scholar Alfred Loisy observed that Jesus came promising the kingdom, but all He left behind was the Church. Loisy was disappointed by this turn of events, but the early Christians most certainly were not.

The early Christians knew that there would indeed be a parousia at the end of time, but there was no less a parousia right now, whenever they celebrated the Mass. When Christ comes at the end of time, He will have no less glory than He has whenever He comes to His Church in the Mass. The only difference, then, is in what we see.

Faced with the evidence of the ancient liturgies, skeptics will sometimes resort to psychoanalyzing the ancients. They say that the idea of a "liturgical parousia" was a late development and a coping mechanism for a disappointed Church. But it wasn't late. Gregory Dix notes that it is in

---

[10] Margaret Barker, "Excursus: *Parousia* and the Liturgy," in *The Revelation of Jesus Christ* (Edinburgh: T&T Clark, 2000), 373, emphasis in original.

the very earliest documents; indeed, some scholars estimate that the liturgy of the Didache could have been written no later than A.D. 48.[11] After reviewing all the ancient Eucharistic texts, Jaroslav Pelikan concludes: "The Eucharistic liturgy was not a compensation for the postponement of the *parousia*, but a way of celebrating the presence of one who had promised to return."[12]

After all, it was Jesus Himself Who set such a high level of expectation in the Church; and it was Jesus Himself Who pointed to its imminent fulfillment. Indeed, it was Jesus Who established the Eucharist as an eschatological event—a parousia—a coming of the King and the kingdom. We must not miss the small but significant details in the scriptural accounts of the Last Supper. As Jesus takes the bread and wine, He says to His apostles: "I have earnestly desired to eat this passover with you before I suffer; for I tell you I shall not eat it until it is fulfilled in the kingdom of God. . . . I shall not drink of the fruit of the vine until the kingdom of God comes" (Lk. 22:15–16, 18). As He institutes the sacrament, He institutes the kingdom. A moment later, He is speaking of the kingdom in terms of a "table" (22:27) and a "banquet" (22:30)—language that will recur in the final chapters of the Book of Revelation. If we are looking for familiar apocalyptic language, we will find it aplenty in Luke's account of the Last Supper—but we will find it always expressed in Eucharistic terms. Jesus

---

[11] On the dating of the *Didache*, see Enrico Mazza, *The Origins of Eucharistic Prayer* (Collegeville, MN: The Liturgical Press, 1995), 40–41.
[12] Pelikan, *The Christian Tradition*, 126–27, italics in original.

goes on to speak of apocalyptic trials, in which believers are "sift[ed] like wheat" (22:31).

No less an authority than Joseph Ratzinger has noted that the New Testament's apocalyptic imagery is over-whelmingly liturgical, and the Church's liturgical language is overwhelmingly apocalyptic. "The parousia is the highest intensification and fulfillment of the liturgy," he writes. "And the liturgy is parousia . . . . Every Eucharist is parousia, the Lord's coming, and yet the Eucharist is even more truly the tensed yearning that He would reveal His hidden Glory."[13]

Thy Kingdom Come!

None of this precludes a parousia of Christ at the end of history. Theologians call that "coming" of Christ the "plenary parousia"—not because Christ will have a greater fullness then, but rather because we will be able to behold Him in His fullness, with our senses unveiled. For, since His coming, Christ is present in the world in a way that He was not in the Old Covenant; but He remains veiled in a way that He will not be at the end. The *Catechism* tells us: "The Kingdom of God has been coming since the Last Supper and, in the Eucharist, it is in our midst. The kingdom will come in glory when Christ hands it over to His Father" (no. 2816).

It is interesting to note that the New Testament speaks not of Christ's "return" but of His "coming." In His

---

[13] Joseph Cardinal Ratzinger, *Eschatology* (Washington, DC: Catholic University of America Press, 1988), 201, italics omitted.

Incarnation, He came; and, as He passed from human sight, He promised to sustain His presence forever: "I am with you always, to the close of the age" (Mt. 28:20).

Thus, His parousia—His presence—remains with us, even as we pray for its plenitude. In the same way, we live even now in Christ's kingdom, even though we daily pray "Thy kingdom come." Contrary to Alfred Loisy's retort, Jesus delivered exactly the kingdom He had promised, and He delivered it as the Church. Recall that our Lord compared the kingdom to a dragnet filled with fish and with trash; recall that He compared it to a field full of both weeds and wheat. He could not have been speaking of the fulfillment of the kingdom at the end of time; for then there will be no trash, no weeds, no tears, no mourning, no crying, no pain, nor anything accursed (cf. Rev. 21:4, 22:3). He was speaking about the Church that we know today—the Church that is the kingdom, the kingdom where the King reigns in the Eucharist.

The kingdom is here now, though we do not yet have eyes to see its fullness. Today we know tears and mourning, but in the Mass we still pray with the words that Christians used in the liturgy of the *Didache:* "For the kingdom, the power, and the glory are Yours, now and forever."

The *Catechism* sums it up: "The Church knows that the Lord comes even now in his Eucharist and that he is there in our midst. However, his presence is veiled" (no. 1404).

Judgment Day

The Eucharist is the parousia—the Real Presence. That is the Church's infallible reflection on the scriptural texts. But what difference should this make to us who go to Mass? The *Catechism* works out the implications for Christian belief and behavior (cf. nos. 1373–78). I commend those points to your attention; but I would have you read them in light of Saint Paul's inspired words on the same subject.

To the Christians at Corinth, Paul poses a rhetorical question: "The cup of blessing which we bless, is it not a participation in the blood of Christ? The bread which we break, is it not a participation in the body of Christ?" (1 Cor. 10:16). The word translated as "participation" is the Greek *koinonia*, which means "communion" or "sharing." It has the same root as the word Saint Peter uses when he describes us Christians as "partakers of the divine nature" (2 Pet. 1:4).

As if to emphasize the reality of this presence, Paul goes on, several lines later to tell the story of Jesus' institution of the Eucharist at the Last Supper, replete with the words: "This is my body . . . . This cup is the new covenant in my blood" (cf. 1 Cor. 11:23–25). Quoting Jesus Himself, Paul leaves no doubt as to the substantial change that takes place in this supreme act of Christian worship.

Then, once Paul has established this presence, he evokes the parousia: "For as often as you eat this bread and drink this cup, you proclaim the Lord's death until he comes" (1 Cor. 11:26). This resonates with everything else we have learned of the first generation of Christians. In their liturgy, they prayed *Maranatha!*—"Come, Lord!"— for they were engaged in the liturgy of His coming, His presence, His parousia.

Lest anyone doubt the reality of this presence—lest anyone think that Christ's Eucharistic presence is somehow lacking in "power and glory"—Paul issues a grave and remarkable warning: "Whoever, therefore, eats the bread or drinks the cup of the Lord in an unworthy manner will be guilty of profaning the body and blood of the Lord. . . . For any one who eats and drinks without discerning the body eats and drinks judgment upon himself" (1 Cor. 11:27, 29).

Whenever the New Testament speaks of Christ's coming, it speaks also of His judgment. The Eucharistic parousia is a real presence—Christ coming in power to judge. His power is evident in its effects on those who receive Communion. Paul speaks specifically of those who receive unworthily and so bring judgment upon themselves. "That is why many of you are weak and ill, and some have died" (1 Cor. 11:30). For such unrepentant sinners, the Eucharist is the final coming of Christ; it is the last judgment.

There is, however, an unspoken corollary to Paul's account of the judgment of sinners. With the Eucharistic parousia comes also the judgment of the saints. If Christ's coming means sickness and death to sinners, how much more will His coming mean blessings and health to those who "discern the Lord's body"?

A liturgy of ancient Egypt expressed this well at the very moment of consecration, when it asks God to make every communicant worthy "to receive a medicine of life for the healing of every sickness and . . . not for condemnation."[14]

---

[14] Wordsworth, *Bishop Sarapion's Prayer-Book*, 63.

This echoes the still-older praise of Saint Ignatius of Antioch, who called the Eucharist the "medicine of immortality, the antidote against death."[15]

It is the glorified Christ who comes in the Eucharist, for communion with those who are worthy to receive the gift. For the saints, the judgment of the parousia is everlasting life, a share in Christ's own resurrected flesh. At the end of the second century, Saint Irenaeus could ask: "How can they say that the flesh, which is nourished with the body of the Lord and with his blood, goes to corruption? . . . For the bread, which is produced from the earth, is no longer common bread, once it has received the invocation of God; it is then the Eucharist, consisting of two realities, earthly and heavenly. So also our bodies, when they receive the Eucharist, are no longer corruptible, but have the hope of the resurrection to eternity."[16]

Closer Than You Think

Just before beginning the "little apocalypse" of Matthew's Gospel, Jesus laments over Jerusalem: "Behold, your house is forsaken and desolate. For I tell you, you will not see me again, until you say, 'Blessed is he who comes in the name of the Lord'" (Mt. 23:38–39).

The citizens of Jerusalem did not discern the Body and Blood of our Lord when He came, and so they

---

[15] Saint Ignatius of Antioch, *Letter to the Ephesians,* in *Ancient Christian Writers, Vol. 1: The Epistles of Saint Clement of Rome and Saint Ignatius of Antioch*, trans. James A. Kleist, S.J. (New York: Newman Press, 1946), 68.

[16] Saint Irenaus of Lyons, *Against the Heresies,* as quoted in Mike Aquilina, *The Mass of the Early Christians* (Huntington, IN: Our Sunday Visitor, 2001), 92.

brought judgment upon themselves. This is a sobering thought for a generation that faces a "crisis" in faith in the Real Presence.

Yet the crisis is not necessarily the one that's reflected in survey data. It's a crisis we must all face. Saint Paul's words should remind us that our generation, and every generation, must face the same choice between blessing and judgment, whenever we present ourselves for Holy Communion.

Our Lord promised: "You will not see me again, until you say, 'Blessed is he who comes in the name of the Lord'"—that is, until the parousia. How right it is for the Church to place those words, "Blessed is he who comes in the name of the Lord," on our lips just moments before the Eucharistic consecration in the Mass, just moments before our Lord's Eucharistic parousia.

If our generation does lack faith in the Eucharist, I think we would profit most from a recovery of the biblical teaching on the sacrament and on the parousia, especially as it is reflected in the *Catechism*.

As Catholics, we must dare to take Jesus at His word and accept His promises on His terms. He promised us a glorious kingdom within His own generation—and, even today, we boldly proclaim that He made good on that promise. For all time, He has established His Eucharistic kingdom, the Church.

What Jesus promised and what He delivered are one and the same. He said He was coming soon—and He is! He said the kingdom is near—and it is. It's as near as your local parish, where the King reigns in the Eucharist. O come, let us adore Him!

Chapter Eleven

The Bible Politicized
The Roots and Fruits of Historical Criticism
A Conversation between Scott Hahn and Karl Keating
September, 1996

KEATING: A few moments ago, before the tape started rolling, you said the misuse of historical criticism points to deficient philosophical formation. I want to find out what you mean, but first let's define historical criticism so we know what we're talking about.

HAHN: It's hard to define, but what I mean by "historical criticism" needs to be understood in two ways. First, the methods are analytical tools, and in and of themselves they can be considered neutral. They can be used positively, and they can be used negatively. Second, the actual circumstances in which these tools were developed gives us another and clearer understanding of what historical criticism is, because at root, historical criticism is grounded in a hermeneutic of suspicion—a basic distrust of tradition—and this was self-conscious on the part of those who developed the methods and of the early practitioners of them in Germany and in England and throughout the world.

KEATING: Is there guilt by association here? Should we be on guard against historical criticism because of how it arose and whom it arose from?

HAHN: Yes. There are two points that are significant in my own study as to the rise of historical criticism. First, the Protestant Reformation split Christendom in the 1500s, and nobody really thought it was going to be permanent. Luther and Calvin, for all their zeal and for all their concern for reform in the Church and for all their pride, didn't really believe that what they were doing was going to represent a permanent fragmentation of Christendom.

Second, two generations went by, and in the early 1600s, the Thirty Year's War began, which first involved Germany, and then England and France, until practically all of Europe was engulfed, with Protestants fighting Catholics, and Lutherans fighting Calvinists, and little sub-groups within Lutheranism and Calvinism warring against each other. This went on for decades. People realized that was going to be a permanent state unless a way out was found. In 1648, the Treaty of Westphalia was signed, and, all of a sudden, Europe made a decision: We must privatize religion. The teachings of the Church or Scripture no longer represented the bond by which European nation-states are united.

Distant Roots

KEATING: So do you see this theological conclusion to be really the consequence of a political dilemma?

HAHN: Yes. In many ways the historical-critical methods began to rise as a sophisticated but subtle rationalization of the state of affairs brought about by the disintegration of the Christian family that was once Christendom. Benedict Spinoza, a Jew excommunicated from the synagogue; Richard Simon, a priest expelled from the Oratorians; Thomas Hobbes, whose work was condemned by his fellow Protestants and the House of Commons—these three men were, for all practical purposes, the founding fathers of historical criticism—Spinoza first.

KEATING: Normally, we don't think of historical criticism as going that far back. Normally we think of it going back maybe to the eighteenth century.

HAHN: Indeed, but more and more contemporary historical critics, such as the German scholar H. G. Reventlow, now point to these founding figures and their joint efforts to show Europe how to bridle religious passions by relativizing, that is, privatizing religious truth claims. As Spinoza asserted, no longer should we be looking at Scripture to find divine truth. Instead, we look to find the meaning intended by the human authors. That's how to drive a wedge between the truth, which binds all people, and the meaning that the authors believed.

KEATING: Was Spinoza trying to effect a civil religion that could keep the political peace while allowing for private variance?

HAHN: He tried to create a natural civil religion by subordinating theological method and religious truth claims to the categories of philosophy. It wasn't simply the elevation of reason over revelation. It was a pitting of reason against faith. The marriage that had endured for many centuries throughout Europe—the marriage of reason and faith based on divine revelation—was split, seemingly forever.

KEATING: The question was at this point, if they can't be married, which is going to be superior? And Spinoza and the others said it should be reason instead of faith.

HAHN: Exactly. In the seventeenth and eighteenth centuries, with the rise of the Enlightenment, you have rationalism on the Continent and empiricism in Great Britain, until Hume's skepticism engulfs all of Europe—leaving Kant to pick up the pieces by turning the mind away from reality, and into itself and its own impression of experiential phenomena. One could almost say that, by reshaping the mind of Europe, Kant rules from the grave. He has shaped a civilization that is, at root, post-Christian.

KEATING: And highly political, as we see even in historical criticism.

HAHN: As Robert and Mary Coote readily demonstrate in *Power, Politics, and the Making of the Bible*, historical-critical methods are employed to find political motives behind the narrative text—for instance, when you divide up the Pentateuch into four sources (*J, E, D*, and *P*). *J*, the Jahwist, supposedly was a tenth-century monarchist who supported the Davidic regime down south, in Judah; whereas *E*, the Elohist, was a representative of the Northern Kingdom, made up of the ten tribes that had revolted against the Davidic empire. The narrative stories in Genesis that seem to support the Davidic monarchy are ascribed to *J*, while the stories that would tend to support the revolutionary policies of the northern tribes that formed the Israelite kingdom are ascribed to *E*.

Of course, the cultic, ritual, and sacrificial ceremonies are identified with the much later source *P*, since they represent the interests of the priestly editors who, after the Babylonian exile, took Jerusalem and built a theocracy under their own control with a priestly monopoly maintained by the very rituals that their rewritten Bibles now stipulated. (This is nothing but Realpolitik.)

As scholars (such as J. D. Leveson at Harvard) point out, many historical critics simply read political interests into ordinary historical discourse, when in fact their conclusions simply reflect their personal political outlook—their own anti-Judaism, for instance as in the case of German scholars of the 1800s, but also a deeply embedded anti-Catholicism.

You'll find Julius Wellhausen doesn't even make an attempt to hide his animus against Roman Catholicism. He sees Jewish ritual in the Old Testament as an ugly precursor to medieval Catholicism.

Albert Schweitzer made a similar observation about the many lives of Jesus written by New Testament Gospel critics: Staring down the well (of history), what they take for the face of Jesus is nothing but their own reflection at the bottom.

Bismarck Backs New Criticism

KEATING: So you've got a political motivation from which you make conclusions about the origin and editing of the Bible. You've declined in dignity by going from the theological or historical to the merely political; you are intruding eighteenth-century thoughts onto the ancient writers.

HAHN: This continued on into the nineteenth century.

KEATING: Under Bismark, we see the Kulturkampf (culture war) and the battle for the unification in Germany. During this time, comes the advance of the historical-critical method in the more modern sense, led by German scholars—all Protestant or at least token Protestant.

HAHN: William Farmer, a world-class New Testament scholar at the University of Dallas, has done a lot of investigation into the Kulturkampf, to discover why it was that the two-source theory—Marcan priority—which a small minority had argued for unsuccessfully in the first half of the nineteenth century, suddenly began taking German scholarship by storm in the 1870s.

Farmer points to the political circumstances surrounding the Kulturkampf, with the definition of papal infallibility in 1870 and Bismarck's reaction. I've been reading about the measures that were administered to suppress the Catholics in Germany, and I don't think many of us realize that the German liberals were hailing Bismarck as a second Luther, especially in driving the Jesuits out and suppressing religious orders. At the time all theology professors were paid by the state, so the shortcut to promotion was by supporting a theory that undermined the proof text used by the papacy to justify its infallibility, Matthew 16:17–19. If Mark's Gospel is first, then the historical reliability of the famous Petrine primacy text is more easily attacked—indeed, scholars were denying its historicity, since it was politically correct to do so.

KEATING: So German scholars in the pay of the state were able to advance precisely to the extent that they came out against the Catholic Church, which Bismarck had a political animus against anyway. The state, indirectly at least, was subsidizing an anti-Catholic exegetical position.

HAHN: Along with anti-Catholic political measures. Here's what Kurt Reinhardt says in *Germany: Two Thousand Years:* "All religious orders and congregations were dissolved. The Catholics' right to organizational assembly was greatly restricted. The Catholic press was subjected to rigorous censorship. Many of the Catholic priests were fined, expelled, or imprisoned."[1]

---

[1] Kurt F. Reinhardt, *Germany: 2000 Years*, vol. 1 (New York: Frederick Ungar Publishing, 1966), 612.

These contemporary political circumstances shed more light on the critics themselves, and the ulterior motives underlying their theories, than whatever light which the critics may throw upon the biblical text—with their alleged discoveries and speculations, which often amounted to little more than hypothetical reconstructions of the pre-history of the text anyway. Instead of focusing on the text itself, they were more concerned, or preoccupied, with discovering the hidden political agendas of the Marcan community, Matthean community, Johannine community—whereas the basic task and primary responsibility of the exegete should be the interpretation of the text as it stands, that is, in its final canonical form.

KEATING: Do you really see those supposed communities of the first century as being projections, or even fantasies, if I can go that far, of eighteenth and nineteenth-century German scholars?

HAHN: Yes, in part. When you study someone like F. C. Bauer, who was greatly influenced by Hegel's dialectic, there's no question that he creates a New Testament theology based on the notion that you've got the Petrine-Jewish church as the thesis, the Pauline-Hellenistic church as the antithesis, and, by the end of the first century, the Johannine community emerges as the synthesis. Nice and tidy, but entirely contrived.

KEATING: When did this idea of Paul against Peter show up? Was it an invention?

HAHN: No, but it's an exaggeration, a total distortion of what is described in Galatians 2, where there was tension between Paul and Peter. But Bauer insists that the New

Testament writers are really suppressing a much bigger conflict, so the conflicting interests must be exposed by Hegel's dialectic.

Whatever conflict existed between Peter and Paul is magnified a hundredfold and made the basis of an elaborate theory of historical development. This amounts to little more than a very imaginative—but purely hypothetical—reconstruction.

KEATING: It's also a cheeky extrapolation. What we find in Galatians 2 is Paul upbraiding Peter in one private setting, and that's pretty much the extent of it. Now, I can understand how a Fundamentalist uses that to argue against papal infallibility rather weakly. But, if you're this nineteenth-century German theologian, you're trying to read into that little story a contest in the early Church between two big camps. Didn't anybody stand up and say, "This emperor has no clothes?"

Cutting-Edge Scholars Sidelined

HAHN: There were several scholars who did, but they were marginalized—Protestants mostly, like E. W. Hengstenberg, but some Catholics too. It's one of those situations where, if you dare to say things that are politically incorrect, your career is ruined. You're blacklisted, you're not promoted, and you certainly will find it much harder to publish.

KEATING: Just like today. As Yogi Berra put it, "It's déjà vu all over again."

HAHN: What we're experiencing in the American Catholic scene, especially in the area of biblical scholarship, is a reflection of, a continuation of, this phenomenon.

KEATING: Cutting-edge scholars who question these things are being marginalized. Their books don't get reviewed, they don't get promoted, and the centers of this scholarship—certain universities—invite onto their staff only people who already agree with the majority opinion. It seems that they're more interested in maintaining this dike against leaks than in seeing whether there's some substance.

HAHN: This phenomenon is especially prevalent in American Catholic scholarly circles. But you seem to find many more Jewish and Protestant scholars doing what Cardinal Ratzinger called for in his 1988 Erasmus Lecture, that is, a "criticism of the critics"—and their misuse of historical-critical methods. And you don't need to look very far to find their vested interests and ulterior motives, their hidden agendas behind their hypothetical reconstructions, and why these tenuous theories catch fire and become the rage of the day. But in Catholic circles you don't find the same sort of thing, at least in North America. Yet Ratzinger's lecture was a clarion call to do precisely this, to recognize the real but limited value of historical criticism: limited uses, but almost unlimited abuses.

KEATING: How was he received by the establishment here?

HAHN: There was official, polite applause.

KEATING: You can't insult a cardinal. Did it amount to "Thank you very much, sir, for your opinion"—and then we just go on doing what we are doing?

HAHN: Perhaps so. From talking with someone who attended, I learned there was polite applause, followed by an awkward silence.

Mired Down?

KEATING: Let's turn now to the Jesus Seminar that has been in the news for much of the year.

HAHN: *Newsweek, Time,* and *U.S. News* came out with cover stories during Holy Week, and they featured the Jesus Seminar, which is extremely radical, but they also highlighted the more moderate views of Father Meier, who is a priest of the Archdiocese of New York and a leading New Testament scholar at a prominent Catholic university.

Father Meier had an opportunity to respond to the Jesus Seminar, and in many ways his response was to the point, but much of what he said left a bit to be desired. We're used to hearing about the Jesus of history and the Christ of faith. But Father Meier is doing something different. He's driving a wedge between the Jesus of history and the historical Jesus, insisting that historical critics can only investigate the historical Jesus. The Jesus of history is a much larger figure, but we're not able to retrieve him through historical-critical methods. So the historical Jesus is nothing more than the Jesus that the critics are capable of recreating with their limited methods.

KEATING: That is, by looking directly at Scripture alone, like Protestants do.

HAHN: Perhaps there's a bit of a *sola scriptura* approach, but it's not just that. The Jesus of history is the real Jesus, the Jesus you would have encountered in the first century. The historical Jesus is the Jesus the practitioners of the historical-critical methods must be content with, nothing more.

KEATING: Is there any way we can reach back and find the Jesus of history?

HAHN: In Father Meier's methodology, no. The ideal he envisions is a Catholic, a Jew, and a Protestant, all biblical scholars, trapped in the basement of Harvard's library, and they aren't allowed out until they reach consensus.

KEATING: This seems reminiscent of John Rawls in his political philosophy a quarter century ago.

HAHN: A "lowest common denominator" approach. Father Meier says we have to begin with the concession that the Gospels have limited value as historical records.

KEATING: This is just an assumption on his part.

HAHN: Not just an assumption, really. He reaches his conclusion using the hermeneutic of suspicion. In the field, he is considered a moderate; at some points, even a conservative. As a Catholic, he says he must conclude his historical-critical studies by saying that Christ was probably born in Nazareth, not Bethlehem.

In a presidential address to the Catholic Biblical Association, Father Meier argued on historical-critical grounds that Jesus had four brothers and at least two sisters, presumably through Mary.[2]

---

[2] See Rev. John P. Meier, "The Brothers and Sisters of Jesus in Ecumenical Perspective," *Catholic Biblical Quarterly* 54 (1992): 1–28. For a concise but insightful critique of Fathers Meier's methodological and philosophical presuppositions, see J. Augustine DíNoia, review of *A Marginal Jew: Rethinking the Historical Jesus* by John P. Meier, *Pro Ecclesia* 2 (Winter, 1993): 122–25. Another helpful critique is offered by Joseph T. Lienhard, in *The Bible, the Church, and Authority* (Collegeville, MN: The Liturgical Press, 1995), 1–8, who delineates some basic flaws in Father Meier's biblical method, including the fact that it is not quite as objective as it claims to be (cf. 7). For additional material, see Roch Kereszty, "Historical Research, Theological Inquiry, and the Reality of Jesus: Reflections on the Method of J. P. Meier," *Communio* 19 (1992): 576–600; Avery Cardinal Dulles, "Historians and the Reality of Christ," *First Things* 28 (December 1992): 20–25; and Rev. Richard J. Neuhaus, "Reason Public and Private: The Pannenberg Project," *First Things* 21 (March 1992): 55–60.

KEATING: The standard Protestant approach.

HAHN: What made it so ironic was that the *Catholic Biblical Quarterly* then published a response by an Evangelical Protestant scholar in England, Richard Bauckham, arguing for one of the traditional Catholic approaches to understanding the brethren of the Lord. He said that the brethren might have been offspring from a previous marriage of Joseph.[3]

But in the *U.S. News* article, the reporter describes how Father Meier keeps his academic work and his faith separate. He says, "You can't mix theology and historical research without causing tremendous confusion."[4] For me that's the issue. Father Meier drives a wedge—a methodological separation—between his faith and theological beliefs on the one hand, and his historical-critical conclusions on the other.

It Wasn't Always This Way . . .

KEATING: Is this the proper method for scholars?

HAHN: I don't think so. After reading the article, I went back and began scouring decades of back issues of the *Catholic Biblical Quarterly* to see how far back this tendency could be traced. I discovered Father J. P. O'Donnell gave a presidential address to the Catholic Biblical Association in 1950. It was published in the *Catholic*

---

[3] Richard Bauckham, "The Brothers and Sisters of Jesus: An Epiphanian Response to John P. Meier," *Catholic Biblical Quarterly* 56, (1994): 686–700.
[4] Rev. John P. Meier, as quoted in Jeffrey L. Sheler, Mike Tharp, and Jill Jordan Sieder, "In Search of Jesus," *U.S. News and World Report* (April 8, 1996), 46–50, 52–53.

Biblical Quarterly the next year, in 1951. He stated: "Certainly then it would never be consonant with the Catholic spirit or tradition to approach the study of Scripture with an attitude of scientific neutrality detached from theological faith. . . . This further attitude does not mean we can contemplate the sacred text in an attitude of faith and be absolved from the duty of continued application to the problems of text, language, history, and archaeology."[5]

But to separate, as Father Meier does, the historical-critical study of Scripture from theological faith is something that, in 1950, the president of the Catholic Biblical Association regarded as unthinkable for authentic Catholic exegetes. Yet now it seems to be the operating assumption.

KEATING: Are we seeing a replay of the philosophical position that is said to have infected some of the Muslim scholars in the Middle Ages? There was a disjuncture between what you believed in faith and what you understood by reason. Through the historical-critical method, the Catholic scholar may say, "This is what really happened"; but, because of his faith, he says, "Actually, it happened this other way." There is an opposition.

HAHN: That's right.

Building Bridges

KEATING: How does he square it? Is the critic saying that both things are true?

---

[5] Rev. Joseph P. O'Donnell, "Presidential Address," *Catholic Biblical Quarterly* 13 (April 1951): 118.

HAHN: He is saying that certain things we conclude from historical-critical research can be at odds with what we believe through faith. This, I believe, is a modern version of the double-truth theory advocated by the thirteenth-century Averroist philosophers. As Chesterton points out in *The Dumb Ox*, Saint Thomas was always polite with his enemies except when it came to Christian Averroists, such as Siger of Brabant, a Catholic scholar who advocated this double-truth approach to knowledge. Aquinas saw in Siger a greater threat to the faith than the Islamic Averroists who attacked it.

KEATING: If I were to use Father Meier's methodology, I could say that, based on historical-critical reasoning, Mary was not perpetually a virgin—she had at least six other children besides Jesus—but through faith I know the Church teaches infallibly that she always was a virgin and Jesus was her only child. I can hold both ideas simultaneously, but what does that do to me mentally? What consequences follow as I deal with the rest of the faith?

HAHN: An erosion process begins, if not in your own lifestyle, then in that of your students, not least in their faith.

KEATING: What's the motivation behind this hermeneutic?

HAHN: Personally, I'm convinced that it's mostly due to peer pressure, wanting to look smart and objective to your fellow scholars, especially non-Catholics. There's also a genuine concern to build bridges, to find common ground with non-Catholic scholars—a fine and worthy motive. But it shouldn't be allowed to control your research, or it ends up becoming a diluted apologetic that is quite ineffective.

KEATING: Bridges to everybody, except to the Magisterium of the Church?

HAHN: Indeed! In contrast, I would say, don't be duplicitous. Just tell other scholars, "Look, I believe these Catholic things, not just with part of my brain, but with all of my mind and with all of my heart, and so they're going to illuminate, they're going to inform, they're going to strengthen my use of the historical method and the critical methods."

Intellectual Schizophrenia

KEATING: This is the response that Jacob Neusner gives in *A Rabbi Talks with Jesus*. He says something like, "You must accept our disagreements. To the extent you try to paint them over, to pretend they aren't there, you insult me. You do not accept me for what I am and what I believe. You think I'm not mature enough to agree to disagree. In trying to build ecumenical bridges to other people, these Catholic exegetes say I should keep off-loading Catholic distinctives until we reach commonality."

HAHN: That's right. It's basically a subtle form of intellectual schizophrenia. People say they believe with one side of the brain what they're denying with the other.

KEATING: That reminds me of the bumper sticker that says, "I'm not schizo, and I'm not either."

HAHN: Indeed. I would say, just to pull things together at this point, that the misuse of historical criticism is practically always based upon inadequate philosophical formation. If people were schooled in the philosophy of Saint Thomas the way Leo XIII intended scholars to be, I think the problem would practically disappear overnight.

It's very important to distinguish between the classical historical method on the one hand, and historical-critical methods that have arisen in the last few centuries. This is a distinction that is seldom made, but, once made and explained, it becomes virtually self-evident.

Going back into antiquity, courts have sifted through documentary sources for evidence, which they have weighed using objective criteria. That is what is meant by the historical method in the classical sense, where you have eyewitness testimony, but only in documentary form.

You ask, were they eyewitnesses? That's the criterion of reliability. Are the eyewitnesses consistent? That's the criterion of consistency. Are the reports whole and intact? That's the criterion of integrity. If these three tests are met, we have to give these eyewitnesses the benefit of the doubt. They were alive then; we weren't. What they're reporting ought to be accepted as *prima facie* evidence. That's the historical method; that's historical research. You can find this basic approach in Louis Gottschalk's *Understanding History*.[6]

But this was overturned with the Enlightenment, with the advent of historical criticism based upon a hermeneutic of suspicion. Indeed, Ernst Troeltsch, the father of historicism, came up with three alternative criteria, his so-called axioms of historical criticism: the principle of *analogy*, so that the past always resembles the present; the idea of

---

[6] Louis Gottschalk, *Understanding History: A Primer of Historical Method* (New York: Knopf, 1969). For a more extensive treatment of the distinction and relationship between the historical method and historical criticism, see Gilbert J. Garraghan, *A Guide to Historical Method* (New York: Fordham University Press, 1957), 33–69.

correlation, which is that you always look for natural causes behind whatever event you're studying; and the principle of *criticism*, that you have a systematic distrust of the reports of tradition and especially of authority.

The point is that if you understand the principles that are behind the historical-critical methods—as distinct from the historical method—you'll see that historical criticism is inherently and intrinsically incapable of proving a supernatural event took place.

KEATING: An analogy: Science cannot prove the Real Presence of Jesus in the Eucharist.

HAHN: Right, and historical-critical methods cannot prove that a miracle occurred. The critical methods are incapable of determining that. Another thing I want to emphasize is that historical critics have not achieved consensus on any single passage of either the Old Testament or the New Testament. They've had two centuries now. They've had thousands of books, tens of thousands of articles, yet they have not achieved consensus. You might have the momentary illusion of consensus (the so-called assured results of modern critical scholarship), but then a new doctoral dissertation comes out and obliterates it. The methods themselves have produced only negative results.

Some critics might respond that they have achieved consensus on some things—that Moses didn't write the Pentateuch, that Isaiah didn't write the second half of his book, that Matthew didn't write first. These are purely negative results used to attack the testimony of tradition. In the case of the Gospels, we have the witness of people who were alive at the time of events they describe. These people wrote when others, still living, could have denied their reports—but didn't. You don't make things up under such circumstances.

Chesterton describes tradition as the democracy of the dead. We're not letting the witnesses speak; we're not allowing tradition to testify. And that's bad science. The results are not only negative, but skeptical. We should interrogate these critics and ask them, "What is it about your methods that renders them incapable of producing interpretive consensus on any single text of the Bible?"

KEATING: Have any of the historical critics tried to answer that question?

HAHN: Not that I know of. It's one of those questions people generally avoid raising in public.

KEATING: John Robinson, in his book, *Redating the New Testament*, said that he wanted to take a fresh look at the dates assigned to the New Testament books. He said the historical-critical method had been running in circles—one scholar footnoting a friend, who footnotes the original scholar, back and forth, back and forth. So Robinson took a fresh look and came up with something close to a traditional Catholic understanding.

HAHN: And I think he did it with scientific integrity and with a degree of scholarly rigor. I don't agree with all his conclusions, but I am generally persuaded by many of the arguments he advanced for a pre-70 dating of the New Testament books.

KEATING: What do you think of the more recent writings of Claude Tresmontant and the late Jean Carmignac?

HAHN: I haven't studied them closely enough to form a final judgment about their conclusions, but I have great respect for their position.

The Ratzinger Gambit

KEATING: Is there a positive role for historical criticism?

HAHN: It's important for Catholics to acknowledge that these methods can be useful so long as we are well-grounded philosophically. Historical criticism functions like a prosecuting attorney. He should be allowed his time to cross-examine witnesses, to impugn motives and to look for vested interests and hidden agendas. Ultimately, when the jury is sent out, if the eyewitnesses have withstood the tests, then the events to which they have testified ought to be accepted. Decisions ought to be reached on their testimony. But if the prosecuting attorney is allowed to create a purely adversarial approach to truth, and if he is allowed to control the outcome, then the courtroom procedure is skewed.

Cardinal Ratzinger describes how the critical methods are analytical tools, and their usefulness depends on the way in which they are used and on the philosophical assumptions that lie behind their use. There is no such thing as the purely neutral use of historical-critical methodology. Instead, what you have is the historical-critical methods being employed according to a particular philosophical outlook. We need to ask, "Which theory has to interfere with the sources the least?"

KEATING: What do you mean interfere?

HAHN: As Ratzinger points out in *Behold the Pierced One*, we ought to prefer the theory that can explain the document as it stands in its final form. Scientifically speaking, the more tenable theory is the one that can explain the document as a whole; the less tenable explains only by chopping up the document into disjointed, even contradictory, sources.

KEATING: In olden times we tried to save the appearances—what accounts most simply for the apparent movement of the sun, planets, and stars around the earth? Ancient and medieval thinkers settled on cycles and epicycles, mathematical constructs that predicted movements in a geocentric system. Later, in a heliocentric system, the appearances were saved through ellipses. Overarching unity again was preserved. You didn't end up with scientists saying Mars moves along a circle, Venus along a square, and Jupiter along a squiggle. The planets weren't deconstructed.

HAHN: Indeed. The more a scholar's interpretive view respects the corpus as given, as a whole—whether the corpus under study is the Book of Genesis, or the entire Pentateuch, or the three synoptic Gospels—the more his view allows the corpus to remain integral.

KEATING: Is this methodology something unique in the application to Scripture? Do scholars employ it in regard to other things? I remember Ronald Knox had a wonderful satire on using the historical-critical method to investigate Alfred Lord Tennyson's poem, "In Memoriam." After tearing it apart line by line and working up fanciful historical and political connection, he concludes that the real author of the poem was Queen Victoria!

HAHN: I'm not surprised.

Reliably Unreliable Conclusions

KEATING: You said earlier that scholars using the historical-critical method often end up with interpretations that are not reliable.

HAHN: Consider the scholar who says, "In this epistle Paul contradicts what he says in another epistle." I would say, let's look for an alternate theory that reveals a deeper logic and intelligibility of seemingly opposed passages.

KEATING: These scholars fall into an error similar to fundamentalist proof-texting, looking too narrowly at something and therefore seeing a conflict. If they took a broader view, there might be no conflict at all.

HAHN: Yes, but there's more. The philosophy behind these methods is alien to the subject matter of the documents.

KEATING: Elaborate on that.

HAHN: You need a critical sympathy, a critical empathy, with the ancient writer whose documents you're studying.

KEATING: Does that mean you have to be a believer?

HAHN: It doesn't mean you have to be a believer, but it implies that a believer has a certain edge.

KEATING: All things being equal, it's better to be a believer than not, when using this scholarship.

HAHN: Being a believer, you're going to approach scriptural texts with critical sympathy. You're going to be more open to finding inner cohesion. You're going to be more capable of achieving a synthesis.

KEATING: Let's conclude our conversation with your prognostication of the future of the historical-critical methods. You've noted that they've been employed with no one verse being resolved with a congenial interpretation by all these exegetes. Is this tank of gas going to run out, or is this car fated to roll on perpetually?

HAHN: I don't see it going away, at least not in the near future or as a result of direct assault. The way to drive out darkness is to turn on the light. I'm convinced that the more the light of faith is turned on for faithful Catholics through solid biblical preaching, teaching, and study, the more a hermeneutic of faith will establish its own scientific and critical superiority in our minds.

KEATING: Will the historical-critical methodology at length wear itself out?

HAHN: The constant misuse of historical criticism is sterile. It doesn't reproduce itself, and so it's dying. It's also parasitical, though, so we've got to be mindful of how it preys upon Catholic students who aren't formed adequately in philosophy.

KEATING: Do you see an end-run being made around the troubles brought on by misuse of the method?

HAHN: I see people appropriating Scripture in terms of our tradition in a wide variety of ways: daily contemplation of the lectionary texts; Bible study faithful to the Magisterium; memorization of key texts of Scripture; the faithful proclamation of the Word by priests. As these expand, the inevitable outcome will be the gradual dissolution of what future generations may regard as twentieth-century "hysterical" criticism.

Chapter Twelve

"O Wondrous Depths!"*
On the Unique Importance and Relative Primacy of Scripture in Catholic Teacihng

When the *Catechism of the Catholic Church* first appeared in 1992, certain scholars immediately cast doubt upon its use of Scripture. One theologian went so far as to charge that "the Catechism quotes Scripture in a fundamentalist way."[1]

We'd gain little by trying to refute such a sweeping generalization, especially since it was asserted without any real evidence. Indeed, the accuser's real problem seems to stem from a one-sided devotion to the real but very limited value of the historical-critical interpretation of Scripture.

The *Catechism* needs no defense from me. I would prefer, instead, to examine the foundations on which rest the *Catechism* and all other Church teaching. I would like to examine the basic framework within which the Church understands Scripture as the divinely inspired Word of God.

---

* "O wondrous are the depths of your words, for see, their surface lies before us, giving delight to your little ones. But wondrous is their depth, O my God, wondrous is their depth!" Saint Augustine, *Confessions*, bk. 12, ch. 14, no. 18.
[1] Elizabeth A. Johnson, C.S.J., "Jesus Christ in the Catechism," *America* 162 (March 3, 1990): 208.

My point of departure is provided by the official statement on "The Use of Sacred Scripture," published as part
of the Informative Dossier of the *Catechism*'s Editorial
Commission in June 1992. After clarifying "that the
Catechism does not want to be a study of scientific exegesis
nor does it intend to present any exegetical hypotheses,"
it states:

> Although aware of these difficulties, today particularly
> serious, that the correct use of Sacred Scripture presents,
> the editors sought to adhere to the methodology indicat-
> ed by [the Second Vatican Council's] *Dei Verbum*, and in
> particular to the *analogia scripturae*. This involves that a
> scripture text be read and interpreted, with the help of
> the Holy Spirit, in the organic unity of the whole of
> Sacred Scripture, whose principal author is God who
> "chose certain men who, all the while he employed them
> in this task, made full use of their powers and faculties,
> so that, though he acted in them and by them, it was as
> true authors that they consigned to writing whatever he
> wanted written, and no more" (*Dei Verbum* 11).[2]

In the first half of this chapter, I'll briefly consider what
it means for God to be the principal author of Scripture
alone. In the second half, I'll examine recent magisterial
teachings on the "referential language" of the inspired
Word, in order to point out Scripture's unique capability
for providing the theological foundation and doctrinal
framework for Catholic theology and catechesis.

---

[2] Editorial Commission of the *Catechism of the Catholic Church*, Informative
Dossier (June 25, 1992), italics and citation in original; http://www.usccb.org.

Only Scripture Is Divinely Inspired and Authored

The Church's perennial teaching is that all Scripture is divinely inspired. In the technical sense, that means that God is its principal author (cf. 2 Tim. 3:16, literally "God-breathed").[3] This doctrine is basic for understanding how the Bible is perceived and interpreted within Catholic tradition. Article 11 of *Dei Verbum* neatly sums this up:

> Those divinely revealed realities which are contained and presented in Sacred Scripture have been committed to writing under the inspiration of the Holy Spirit. For holy mother Church, relying on the belief of the Apostles (see Jn. 20:31; 2 Tim. 3:16; 2 Pet. 1:19–20; 3:15–16), holds that the books of both the Old and New Testaments in their entirety, with all their parts, are sacred and canonical because written under the inspiration of the Holy Spirit, they have God as their author and have been handed on as such to the Church herself. In composing the sacred books, God chose men and while employed by Him they made use of their powers and abilities, so that with Him acting in them and through them, they, as true authors, consigned to writing everything and only those things which He wanted.

> Therefore, since everything asserted by the inspired authors or sacred writers must be held to be asserted by the Holy Spirit, it follows that the books of Scripture

---

[3] The bibliography on the subject of biblical inspiration is vast. The best overview of the Church's traditional teaching is still C. Pesch, S.J., *De inspiratione Sacrae Scripturae* (Freiburg: Herder, 1906).

must be acknowledged as teaching solidly, faithfully and without error that truth which God wanted put into sacred writings for the sake of salvation (*DV*, 11).[4]

---

[4] *Dei Verbum* (11 n. 4) cites Pope Leo XIII's Encyclical on the Study of Holy Scripture *Providentissimus Deus* [(November 18, 1893), hereafter cited as *PD*; see also *Enchiridion Biblicum: Documenta Ecclesiastica Sacram Scripturam Spectantia*, 4th ed. (Naples & Rome, 1961), hereafter cited as *EB*]. In article 20 of *Providentissimus Deus*, Pope Leo XIII states: "For all the books which the Church receives as sacred and canonical, are written wholly and entirely, with all their parts, at the dictation of the Holy [Spirit]; and so far is it from being possible that any error can coexist with inspiration, that inspiration is not only essentially incompatible with error, but excludes and rejects it as absolutely and necessarily as it is impossible that God Himself, the supreme Truth, can utter that which is not true. This is the ancient and unchanging faith of the Church" (*EB*, 125). Also noteworthy is the statement in the immediately preceding paragraph: "But it is absolutely wrong and forbidden either to narrow inspiration to certain parts only of Holy Scripture, or to admit that the sacred writer has erred. For the system of those who, in order to rid themselves of these difficulties, do not hesitate to concede that divine inspiration regards the things of faith and morals, and nothing beyond . . . this system cannot be tolerated" (*PD*, 20; *EB*, 124).

Twice *Dei Verbum* cites Pope Pius XII, in his Encyclical on Promoting Biblical Studies *Divino Afflante Spiritu* [(September 30, 1943), hereafter cited as *DAS*] on two significant points. First, on the Thomistic distinction between principal and instrumental authorship, precisely at the point where Pope Pius XII gives a ringing endorsement of Saint Thomas's explanatory theory of instrumentality to explain the mystery of concurrence in the dual authorship of Scripture (*DV*, 11 n. 2):

Among these it is worthy of special mention that Catholic theologians, following the teaching of the Holy Fathers and especially of the Angelic and Common Doctor, have examined and explained the nature and effects of biblical inspiration more exactly and more fully than as wont to be done in previous ages. For having begun by expounding minutely the principle that the inspired writer, in composing the sacred book, is the living and reasonable instrument of the Holy Spirit, they rightly observe that, impelled by the divine motion, he so uses his faculties and powers, that from the book composed by him all may easily infer "the special character of each one and, as it were, his personal traits" (*DAS*, 33; *EB*, 556).

The Holy Spirit is at work in the Scriptures and in the Magisterium—but in different ways. The indefectibility and infallibility of the Church and her teaching office is

---

Second, on the issue of the extent of inerrancy and the authority of Leo XIII's teaching in *Providentissimus Deus*. Here we have very strong statements of Pius XII's solemn endorsement of Leo XIII's teaching on this controversial subject (*DV*, 11 n. 5):

> When, subsequently, some Catholic writers, in spite of this solemn definition of Catholic doctrine, by which such divine authority is claimed for the "entire books with all their parts" as to secure freedom from any error whatsoever, ventured to restrict the truth of Sacred Scripture solely to matters of faith and morals, and to regard other matters whether in the domain of physical science of history, as *"obiter dicta"* and—as they contended—in no wise connected with faith, Our Predecessor of immortal memory, Leo XIII in the Encyclical Letter *Providentissimus Deus*, published on November 18th in the year 1893, justly and rightly condemned these errors and safe-guarded the studies of the Divine Books by the most wise precepts and rules (*DAS*, 1; *EB*, 538).

He refers to Leo XIII's encyclical as "the supreme guide in biblical studies" which he resolves to commemorate for the purpose of safeguarding Scripture studies which "may most opportunely be done ratifying and inculcating all that was wisely laid down by Our Predecessor and ordained by His Successors for the consolidating and perfecting of the work" (*DAS*, 2; *EB*, 538).

Then Pope Pius XII underscores Leo XIII's primary concern:

> The first and greatest care of Leo XIII was to set forth the teaching on the truth of Sacred Books and to defend it from attack. Hence with grave words did he proclaim that there is no error whatsoever if the sacred writer, speaking of things of the physical order, "went by what sensibly appeared" as the Angelic Doctor says, "speaking either in figurative language, or in terms which were commonly used at the time, and which in many instances are in daily use at this day, even among the most eminent men of science." For "sacred writers, or to speak more accurately—the words are Saint Augustine's—the Holy Spirit, Who spoke by them, did not intend to teach men these things—that is the essential nature of the things of the universe—things in no way profitable to salvation"; which principle "will apply to cognate sciences, and especially to history," that is, by refuting, "in a somewhat similar way the fallacies of the adversaries and defending the historical truth of Sacred Scripture from their attacks."

every bit as rooted in the working of the Holy Spirit as is the inspiration of the pages of Scripture. Yet God is at work in each in a different manner (cf. *Catechism*, nos. 80–83).

One thing, however, is often and easily overlooked in all of this. Let's make sure we don't miss it. Notice that Catholic teaching stipulates how the charism of divine inspiration pertains only to Scripture—not to the Church Magisterium or Sacred Tradition. As Pierre Benoit, O.P., explains in his study on *Prophecy and Inspiration*:

> This point may be clarified by a comparison with the charism of infallibility. Infallibility is only a negative assistance, having for its formal object to guarantee against error, and bearing solely on "res fidei et morum" which are subject to the decision of the Church. . . . Inspiration is a positive influence which bears on the entire content of the sacred book, and which, among other effects, guarantees the infallible truth of this content to the extent that God teaches therein. It is, therefore, obvious that the

---

Nor is the sacred writer to be taxed with error, if "copyists have made mistakes in the text of the Bible," or, "if the real meaning of a passage remains ambiguous." Finally, it is absolutely wrong and forbidden "either to narrow inspiration to certain passages of Holy Scripture, or to admit that the sacred writer has erred," since divine inspiration "not only is essentially incompatible with error but excludes and rejects it absolutely and necessarily as it is impossible that God Himself, the supreme Truth, can utter that which is not true. This is the ancient and constant faith of the Church" (*DAS*, 3; *EB*, 539).

Pius XII concludes his purpose statement by clarifying the authority of Leo XIII's teaching: "This teaching, which our Predecessor Leo XIII set forth with such solemnity, We also proclaim with Our authority and We urge all to adhere to it religiously. No less earnestly do We inculcate obedience at the present day to the counsels and exhortations which he, in his day, so wisely enjoined" (*DAS*, 4; *EB*, 540).

infallibility of the Church is not a substitute for inspiration, or a lower order of inspiration, as we are sometimes led to believe; it is a charism of a different order.[5]

Thus, inspiration and infallibility are each distinct charisms, both of which involve some direct influence of the supernatural order. Inspiration is a charism of a higher order, however; it entails "a particularly efficacious determining impulse."[6] The result is the distinctive and singular privilege of inerrancy. Inspiration occurs when God's positive influence is brought to bear upon a human writer to guarantee the truth of each and every one of his intentional affirmations. Thus, inspiration pertains to Scripture alone. On the other hand, infallibility is a lesser charism involving merely a negative assistance, which prevents the authoritative transmission of error solely in matters of faith and morals. As the Magisterium consistently teaches, it is God's positive assistance in inspiring Scripture that causes its inerrancy to cover all of the writer's intentional affirmations of truth. This is why inerrancy cannot be restricted to faith and morals.[7]

---

[5] P. Synave, O.P. and P. Benoit, O.P., *Prophecy and Inspiration*, trans. A. R. Dulles, S.J. and T. L. Sheridan, S.J. (New York: Desclee, 1961), no. 1, 132.

[6] Synave and Benoit, *Prophecy and Inspiration*, 95.

[7] In his commentary on *Dei Verbum*, Augustin Cardinal Bea, who was sent by Pope Paul VI to assist in the final drafting of this difficult section of the Dogmatic Constitution, comments on the extent of the inerrancy as it is set forth in article 11:

> An earlier *schema* (the third in succession) said that the sacred books teach "truth without error." The following *schema*, the fourth, inspired by the words of Saint Augustine, added the adjective "saving," so that

For the sake of clarity, some other distinctions can be made. First, God is identified as the principal author of Scripture, whereas He is not properly the author—but only the guarantor—of the infallible teachings of Tradition and the Magisterium. It is the human writers who function freely and fully as the instrumental authors of Scripture. Second, whereas all three channels of revelation (Scripture, Tradition, and Magisterium) convey the Word of God, Scripture alone consists of God's words. This point is succinctly stated in article 24 of *Dei Verbum:* "For the Sacred Scriptures contain the word of God and

> the text asserted that the Scriptures taught "firmly, faithfully, wholly, and without error the saving truth." In the voting which followed one hundred and eighty-four council fathers asked for the adjective "saving" to be removed, because they feared it might lead to misunderstandings, as if the inerrancy of Scripture referred only to matters of faith and morality, whereas there might be error in the treatment of other matters. The Holy Father, to a certain extent sharing this anxiety, decided to ask the Commission to consider whether it would be better to omit the adjective, as it might lead to some misunderstanding. [Augustin Cardinal Bea, *The Word of God and Mankind* (Chicago: Franciscan Herald Press, 1967), 188, italics in original].

Bea then proceeds to raise the question: "Does the inerrancy asserted in this document cover also the account of these historical events?" To which he answers:

> For my own part I think that this question must be answered affirmatively, that is, that these "background" events also are described without error. In fact, we declare in general that there is no limit set to this inerrancy, and that it applies to all that the inspired writer, and therefore all that the Holy Spirit by his means, affirms. . . . This thought, which re-occurs in various forms in the recent documents of the Magisterium of the Church (cf. EB 124, 279, 450 et. seq., 539 et seq., 559) is here clearly understood in a sense which excludes the possibility of the Scriptures containing any statement contrary to the reality of the facts. In particular, these documents of the Magisterium require us to recognize that Scripture gives a true account of events, naturally not in the sense that it always offers a complete and scientifically studied account,

since they are inspired, really are the word of God, and so the study of the sacred page is, as it were, the soul of sacred theology." Because of divine inspiration, then, everything intentionally affirmed by the human writers of Scripture is also directly spoken by God. Inspired Scripture embodies God's word.

Scripture's "Referential Language"

"The study of the sacred page is . . . the soul of sacred theology"—those words, previously cited, are where we must begin in considering Scripture's "referential nor-

---

sense that it always offers a complete and scientifically studied account, but in the sense that what is asserted in Scripture—even if it does not offer a complete picture—never contradicts the reality of the fact. If therefore the Council had wished to introduce here a new conception, different from that presented in these recent documents of the supreme teaching authority, which reflects the beliefs of the early fathers, it would have had to state this clearly and explicitly. Let us now ask whether there may be any indication to suggest such a restricted interpretation of inerrancy. The answer is decidedly negative. There is not the slightest sign of any such indication. On the contrary, everything points against a restrictive interpretation (Bea, *The Word of God and Mankind*, 189–90, emphasis omitted, citation in original).

Thus, he interprets the grammatical sense of the key phrase, 'for the sake of salvation' by clarifying what it is intended to be linked with: "[I]n fact, the phrasing we now have does not admit of any such [restrictive] interpretation, because the idea of salvation is no longer directly linked with the noun 'truth,' but with the verbal expression 'wanted put into the sacred writings'; in other words, the phrase in which the text speaks of salvation explains God's purpose in causing the Scriptures to be written, and not the nature of the truth enshrined therein" (Bea, *The Word of God and Mankind*, 190–91). Also see the comments made by Bishop Whealon in a written submission made during the course of debate where he admits the difficulties with the inerrancy of Scripture, but considers that they can be solved over time: *"Revera adsunt difficultates praesertim in rebus historiae, sed Spiritu Sancto adiuvante studium et labor oratio exegetarum etiam has difficultates in futurum solvent"* [A. Grillmeier, "The Divine Inspiration and the Interpretation of Sacred Scripture," in *Commentary on the Documents of Vatican II*, vol. 3 (New York: Herder and Herder, 1969), 208].

mativity" for Catholic theology and doctrinal catechesis. Scripture must be the norm. Scripture must be the objective point of reference.

Since the close of Vatican II, the Church has often and emphatically affirmed Scripture's normative role for theology. For instance, four years after the promulgation of *Dei Verbum*, Pope Paul VI states: "In accord with the teachings of the Second Vatican Council, all will thus regard Sacred Scripture as the abiding source of spiritual life, the foundation for Christian instruction, and the core of all theological study."[8]

The Sacred Congregation for Catholic Education makes a similar point in a 1976 document on *The Theological Formation of Future Priests:* "The basic fact which theological teaching must take into account is that Sacred Scripture is the starting point, the permanent foundation, and the life-giving and animating principle of all theology (cf. *DV,* 24)." It then applies this basic fact to the teaching of theology: "The primordial role of Sacred Scripture determines the nature of its relation to theology and its various disciplines. . . . Consequently, after the introductory questions have been handled, the teaching of Sacred Scripture must culminate in a biblical theology which gives a unified vision of the Christian mystery."[9]

---

[8] Pope Paul VI approves the new Roman Missal in *Missale Romanum* (April 3, 1969), in *Documents of the Liturgy* 1969–1979 (Collegeville, MN: Liturgical Press, 1982), DOL 202, 458; see also *Acta Apostolicae Sedis* 61 (1969): 217–22 (hereafter cited *AAS*).

[9] Sacred Congregation for Catholic Education, *The Theological Formation of Future Priests* (February 22, 1976), in *The Pope Speaks* 21 (1976): 365–66, citation in original.

John Paul II shares similar ideas in a 1980 address to theologians at the Lateran University: "Faithfulness means . . . putting the Word of God, which the Church 'listens to religiously' [cf. *DV*, 1], at the very origin of the theological process and referring to it all the acquired knowledge and conclusions gradually reached."[10] He reiterates this basic concern in his 1986 address to the Catholic Faculty of Lyon: "Theology must take its point of departure from a continual and updated return to the Scriptures read in the Church."[11] Clearly, the Magisterium is calling Catholic theologians back to their scriptural roots; perhaps the only question is whether theologians will recognize this magisterial mandate and begin moving in this new direction.

This theological direction is strongly reinforced by an unusually emphatic statement made in a 1984 document from the Pontifical Biblical Commission entitled "Scripture and Christology": "The 'auxiliary' languages employed in the Church in the course of centuries do not enjoy the same authority, as far as faith is concerned, as the 'referential language' of the inspired authors, especially (that) of the New Testament with its mode of expression rooted in the Prior (Testament)."[12] What is meant by the reference to auxiliary languages? Clearly, it refers to the various credal terms (e.g., *homoousios, theotokos, trinitas*), dogmatic concepts (e.g.,

---

[10] Pope John Paul II, Address (February 16, 1980), in "Pope John Paul at the Pontifical Lateran University," *L'Osservatore Romano*, March 15, 1980.

[11] Pope John Paul II, Address (October 7, 1986); *AAS* 79 (1987): 337–38.

[12] Pontifical Biblical Commission, "Scripture and Christology," in J. A. Fitzmyer, S.J., trans., *Scripture and Christology: A Statement of the Biblical Commission with a Commentary* (New York: Paulist Press, 1986), 1.2.2.1, 20; cf. Pontifical Biblical Commission, *Bible et Christologiae* (Paris: Cerf, 1984).

original sin, hypostatic union, Immaculate Conception), and theological methodologies (e.g., Thomism, Scotism, Molinism, scholasticism) that were developed and used to teach true doctrine, quite often in the face of heresy, throughout Church history. These auxiliary languages have proven indispensible for maintaining, defending, and transmitting the Catholic faith in its integrity.

The reference to auxiliary languages also includes terms, concepts, and methods that are presently being developed and employed so that contemporary theology may articulate revelation in a way that is faithful and meaningful to the present age. Like the auxiliary languages developed in the past, those of the present must draw from contemporary philosophical systems with precision and care. No matter how useful these languages may be, in the past or at present, they are subordinate to the divinely inspired language of Scripture which they are created to clarify, explain, and protect in the first place. Consequently, they lack the "referential" authority of the affirmations made by the inspired writers of Scripture. Scripture's "referential language" must be what guides, assists, and judges the efforts of theologians as they develop and employ auxiliary languages.

In the document "Scripture and Christology," two different types of theology are addressed according to the unique dangers they face. First, the document suggests that "classical theology" faces "a certain hazard": "The formulation of doctrine about Christ depends more on the language of theologians of the patristic period and the Middle Ages than on the language of the New Testament itself, as if this ultimate source of the revelation (about him) were less accurate and less suited to setting forth a doctrine in well-defined terms."[13] The document also warns of a certain hazard in adapting modern philosophical systems for christology:

> In this matter the risk is that an absolute value be ascribed to modes of thinking and speaking that are proper to our age, with the result that the understanding of Christ which flows from the Gospels can be called in question. This would certainly be the case if New Testament texts were to be subjected to a selective process or an interpretation that various philosophical systems would call for. But a Christology cannot be solidly worked out unless the equilibrium be preserved that flows from Sacred Scripture taken as a whole and from the various modes of speaking which it employs.[14]

In sum, the auxiliary languages of theology—past and present—should be drawn from the referential language of Scripture, just as their development and use should point people back to Scripture's inspired revelation.

By emphasizing the referential language of Scripture, the Magisterium is not discouraging or devaluing the use of auxiliary languages for systematic theology. This point is apparently lost to some theologians, however, who resist acknowledging the language of Scripture to be referential. In 1986, Roch Kereszty, O.Cist., published an article in *Communio*, "'The Bible and Christology' Document of the

---

[13] Pontifical Biblical Commission, "Scripture and Christology," 1.2.1.1, 19, emphasis omitted.
[14] Pontifical Biblical Commission, "Scripture and Christology," 1.2.2.2, 20–21, emphasis omitted.

Biblical Commission," in which he analyzes the document's statement about the "referential language" of Scripture. He begins by voicing the concern that some may have: "This statement, at first reading, seems to challenge the very existence of systematic christology."[15]

In other words, why bother theologizing about Christ in a contemporary vein if all that is needed is simply to restate the inspired affirmations in Scripture about Christ? According to Kereszty, the document anticipates and addresses this concern with real insight:

> If Scriptural formulas are the most accurate and the best suited for expressing christological doctrine, then why do we need magisterial statements and theological speculation? However, if you place this statement in the context of the whole document, it no longer appears to eliminate systematic christology, but rather profoundly transforms it. Systematic theologians, insists ["Bible and Christology"], will follow the direction given in the New Testament itself (that used Hellenistic terms to express the person and the work of Jesus, in a Hellenistic culture), and will find in every new age and culture new auxiliary languages "in order to make clear for their contemporaries the special and fundamental language of Sacred Scripture" (2.2.2.2/d). Thus further explanations and clarifications are constantly necessary, but their goal is to make accessible to the people of a given age and culture that fullness which is contained in the Scriptures.[16]

---

[15] Roch A. Kereszty, O. Cist., "The 'Bible and Christology' Document of the Biblical Commission," *Communio* 13 (Winter 1986): 363.

[16] Kerestzy, "The 'Bible and Christology' Document," 363, citation in original.

Instead of discouraging systematic christology, the recognition of Scripture's referential authority serves to engage theologians more deeply in the faithful pursuit of critical research. This occurs in at least two stages. First, Scripture shows them how the mystery of Christ may be communicated to people who are ignorant of Scripture by establishing linguistic points of contact between Christ and their culture, like the apostles and New Testament writers did throughout the ancient Roman Empire. Second, Scripture also shows how, after people are introduced to the basic truth of the Gospel, they may be drawn more deeply into the mysteries of faith, as Saint Paul initiated his Gentile converts into Israel's covenant heritage with God—"the sonship, the glory, the covenants, the giving of the law, the worship, and the promises" (Rom. 9:4).

Later in "Bible and Christology," this twofold process is described in relation to Scripture:

> For the inspired authors seek in this way to describe the same Christ that others depict with expressions drawn more directly from the Scriptures themselves. But they have thus opened up a way for theologians of all ages who have felt the need, and still feel it, of finding "auxiliary" languages to clarify for the people of their day the special and basic language of Scripture so that the correct and integral proclamation of the gospel might be brought to human beings of all ages.[17]

---

[17] Kerestzy, "The 'Bible and Christology' Document," 363.

Interestingly, these two actions parallel two crucial stages of the Church's mission: evangelization and catechesis. The Church is thus calling exegetes and theologians to share in its divine vocation to evangelize the Church and the world. We hear this challenging call in the words of Paul VI: "[I]nterpretation has not fulfilled its task until it has demonstrated how the meaning of Scripture may be referred to the present salvific moment, that is, until it has brought out the application to the present circumstances of the Church and the world. Without taking anything away from the value of philological, archeological and historical interpretation of the text—always necessary— we have to lay emphasis on the continuity between exegesis and preaching."[18]

He voices similar ideas in a 1974 address to the Pontifical Biblical Commission: "Your work is not limited . . . to explaining old texts, reporting facts in a critical way or going back to the early and original form of a text or a sacred page. It is the prime duty of the exegete to present to the people of God the message of revelation, to set forth the meaning of the Word of God in itself and in relation to man today."[19] John Paul II insists on the same principle when he addressed the same Commission fifteen years later: "In the Church all methods of exegesis must be, directly or indirectly, at

---

[18] Pope Paul VI, Address (September 5, 1970), no. 1, in "Church Favors Every Attempt to Attain Deeper Understanding of S. Scriptures," *L'Osservatore Romano*, October 8, 1970, emphasis omitted.

[19] Pope Paul VI, Address (March 14, 1974), in "Importance of Biblical Studies for the Ecumenical and Missionary Activity of the Church," *L'Osservatore Romano*, April 18, 1974.

the service of evangelization."[20] The clear implication is that exegetes and theologians are to view their work as united to God's inspired Word written and proclaimed.

This point is easily missed by exegetes and theologians who overlook the fact that the inspired writers of the New Testament were not just apostles and evangelists, but were themselves exegetes and theologians who explored the depths of the revealed mysteries of faith. However, this fact was not overlooked by the Church's leading lights in the patristic and medieval periods. As Joseph Cardinal Ratzinger explains in a lengthy statement that deserves to be cited in full:

Aristotle draws a distinction between *theologia* and *theologike*—between theology and the study of theology. By the first, he distinguished the divine discourse; by the second, human effort to understand the divine. On the basis of this linguistic tradition, pseudo-Dionysius used the word "theology" to designate Holy Scripture; for him, it is what the ancients meant by the word—the discourse of God rendered in human words. In his later years, Bonaventure made this mode of speech his own and, on the basis of it, rethought his understanding of theology as a whole. Properly speaking, God himself must be the subject of theology. Therefore, Scripture alone is theology in the fullest sense of the word because it truly has God as its subject; it does not just speak of him but is his own speech. It lets God himself speak. But Bonaventure does not thereby overlook the fact that this speaking on the part of God is, nevertheless, a human speaking. The

---

[20] Pope John Paul II, Address (April 7, 1989), in "Exegesis Must Serve Evangelization," *L'Osservatore Romano*, (April 17, 1989).

writers of Holy Scripture speak as themselves, as men, and yet, precisely in doing so, they are *"theologoi,"* those through whom God as subject, as the word that speaks itself, enters history. What distinguishes Holy Scripture from all later theology is thus completely safeguarded, but, at the same time, the Bible becomes the model of all theology, and those who are the bearers of it become the norm of the theologian, who accomplishes his task properly only to the extent that he makes God himself his subject . . . . What we have said can now be formulated as the . . . final thesis of these remarks: theology is a spiritual science. The normative theologians are the authors of Holy Scripture. This statement is valid not only with reference to the objective written document they left behind but also with reference to their manner of speaking, in which it is God himself who speaks.[21]

Perhaps Aristotle's distinction can be restated and then applied to the current situation in Catholic theology: while the Magisterium mandates a return to "theology," properly speaking, by studying and adhering to the referential language of inspired Scripture, many seem to prefer a kind of "theologian-ology" that focuses on classical or contemporary theologians. Both are necessary and proper, but the former ought to take precedent over the latter.

Through the charism of inspiration, Scripture has become an integral part of the saving mystery of Christ. As God's Word is united to human nature in Christ, so God's words are united with those of the human writers in

---

[21] Joseph Cardinal Ratzinger, *Principles of Catholic Theology: Building Stones for a Fundamental Theology*, trans. M. F. McCarthy (San Francisco: Ignatius, 1987), 321, italics in original.

Scripture. Accordingly, the divinely inspired discourse that culminates in the New Testament is made to coincide with God's incarnational debut in Christ. Thus, the tightest bond exists between the incarnation of God's Word in Christ and the inspiration of God's Word in Scripture. The two are so interdependent and mutually interpretive that neither one can be truly known without the other. That is what makes the inspired Word so unique: It fully partakes of the mystery that it inerrantly imparts. Thus, it is uniquely capable of providing the theological foundation and doctrinal framework for Catholic theology and catechesis; and this is something upon which the Magisterium insists.

Indeed, the Magisterium has thrown down the gauntlet. What will happen if theologians take it up? Undoubtedly, to do so, systematicians must become thoroughly acquainted with Scripture, and grounded in its covenant theology and salvation history, just as exegetes must be able and willing to teach a style of theological exegesis that builds upon—yet goes beyond—historical-critical exegesis. This point must be made clearly: Catholic exegetes do not need to reject historical-critical methods. But they should only employ these methods with caution; at the same time, they do not have to employ only these methods. The Church recommends cautious but non-exclusive use. Two centuries of practice show limited uses—and virtually unlimited abuses.[22]

---

[22] For a balanced treatment of historical-critical exegesis, see Joseph Cardinal Ratzinger, "Biblical Interpretation in Crisis: On the Question of the

What would happen to ordinary Catholics if this challenge were accepted and the mandate realized? Perhaps the result would be Catholics discovering all the riches and mysteries of their faith within Scripture. Indeed, this is precisely what Catholic catechesis must strive for in the future, as John Paul II forcefully states in his "Apostolic Exhortation on Catechesis in Our Time" (*Catechesi Tradendae*), where he makes a strong plea for restoring the primacy of Scripture to catechesis:

> To speak of Tradition and Scripture as the source of catechesis is to draw attention to the fact that catechesis must be impregnated and penetrated by the thought, the spirit and the outlook of the Bible and the Gospels through assiduous contact with the texts themselves; but it is also a reminder that catechesis will be all the richer and more effective for reading the texts with the intelligence and the heart of the Church and for drawing

---

Foundations and Approaches of Exegesis Today," in *Biblical Interpretation in Crisis: The Ratzinger Conference on the Bible and Church*, ed. Richard John Neuhaus (Grand Rapids: Eerdmans, 1989), 1–23.

Elsewhere, Ratzinger writes:

> The historical-critical method is essentially a tool, and its usefulness depends on the way in which it is used, i.e., on the hermeneutical and philosophical presuppositions one adopts in applying it. In fact, there is no such thing as a pure historical method; it is always carried on in a hermeneutical or philosophical context, even when people are not aware of it or expressly deny it. The difficulties which faith continually experiences today in the face of critical exegesis do not stem from the historical or critical factors as such but from the latent philosophy which is at work. The argument, therefore, must relate to this underlying philosophy; it must not attempt to bring historical thought as such under suspicion [Joseph Cardinal Ratzinger, *Behold the Pierced One: An Approach to Spiritual Christology* (San Francisco: Ignatius, 1986), 43].

inspiration from the two thousand years of the Church's reflection and life.[23]

Unfortunately, many Catholics still feel they must avoid studying Scripture, sometimes because they are confused by difficulties in the text or with critical interpretations of it. In any case, many Catholics still react to the tactics used by aggressive non-Catholic believers—the so-called Bible Christians who teach and practice the Protestant doctrine of *sola scriptura.* By now every Catholic should know—and be able to show—the unscriptural character of this doctrine (cf. 1 Tim. 3:15; 2 Thess. 2:15, 3:6), although it is not beyond rehabilitation (e.g., *solum verbum Dei,* "only the Word of God"; *prima scriptura,* "Scripture first"). Too often, however, Catholics yield to something like an out-of-court divorce settlement: "She gets the house while I keep the car and furniture," becomes, "They get the Scripture while we keep Tradition and the Magisterium." In truth, they are inseparable: Scripture and the Church—both or neither! Thus, the proper interpretation of Scripture must be done in the Church, for the Church, and by the Church. For the Church is the Mystical Body of Christ Who, as its head, sent the Holy Spirit to be the indwelling soul of the Body of Christ. The same Spirit Who inspired the founders and leaders of the Church in the first generation to write the New Testament is able to guide their successors to understand and teach it truly in all future generations. The Holy Spirit enlightens the Church to interpret what He inspired.

[23] Pope John Paul II, Apostolic Exhortation on Catechesis in Our Time *Catechesi Tradendae* (October 16, 1979), no. 27 (hereafter cited in the text as *CT*); see also *Catechesi Tradendae* (Boston: Daughters of Saint Paul, 1979), 23.

Prime Matter

By now it should be clear that *prima scriptura*— "Scripture first"—is not a new idea.[24] The Church has lived by this principle, and theologians have recognized this.

The first time I encountered the notion of *prima scriptura* was in Brian Tierney's famous study on the *Origins of Papal Infallibility.* Indeed, his discussion followed under the subheading "The Primacy of Scripture." Tierney summarizes the views of Guido Terreni, who, in adhering to the teaching of Pope John XXII, held to "a very different point of view" from that of the more novel and radical teachings of the Joachimites and William of Ockham.[25] As Tierney states: "For Guido, then, the church was unerring in its interpretation of Scripture; but Scripture was the essential source of the church's teachings."[26]

The idea is further developed in Cardinal Yves Congar's important work, *Tradition and Traditions*, where he showed how this view of Scripture's normative primacy was common, from the Fathers through Saint Thomas Aquinas: "The Fathers of the Church, and then the medieval theologians, especially Saint Thomas Aquinas, had made the necessary distinction, and it is a fact that, in this whole business, the Thomists were most faithful to the normative primacy of Scripture."[27]

---

[24] It should be noted that *prima scriptura* does not imply the superiority of Scripture, but rather, its relative primacy for Catholic theology.

[25] Brian Tierney, *Origins of Papal Infallibility* (Leiden: E. J. Brill, 1972), 251.

[26] Tierney, *Origins of Papal Infallibility*, 254.

[27] Yves Cardinal Congar, *Tradition and Traditions* (San Diego: Basilica Press, 1997), 175.

Prima scriptura is also reflected in the authoritative commentary on Vatican II's "Dogmatic Declaration on Divine Revelation" *(Dei Verbum)*, written by Cardinal Augustin Bea. Bea states: "This pre-eminence of Holy Scripture, in as much as it is inspired by God, is confirmed in the Council's reason for asserting that the written word of God is the supreme rule of faith . . . . For only inspired writings (cf. no. 11) 'teach firmly, faithfully and without error' the whole truth which God desired to be consigned to writing for our salvation." He also clarifies that Tradition "is not formally the word of God, like Scripture."[28]

Postscript: Spiritual Exegesis and Inculturation

I hope I have demonstrated the Church's teaching on Scripture's referential authority. Still, it's fair for readers to ask what practical difference this makes for Catholic theology and catechesis. To answer this adequately would require a separate study. All we can do in this postscript is make a few suggestions to encourage future research, discussion, writing, teaching and preaching on the subject. In order to keep these suggestions brief, they are simply listed in summary fashion.

1. A Wholehearted Return to Scripture. The fortunes of the Church throughout history depend on her love of Christ and, consequently, her openness to Him speaking through Scripture. The great Catholic Scripture commentator, Cornelius A. Lapide, testifies to the conviction of Saint Teresa of Avila: "S[aint] Teresa, a woman endowed

---

[28] Augustin Cardinal Bea, *The Word of God and Mankind*, 270.

with the spirit of prophecy, and renowed throughout all Spain for the glory of her miracles, and the sanctity of her life, was taught by God that all the troubles of the Church, all the evils in the world, flow from this source, that men do not, by clear and sound knowledge, and serious consideration, penetrate into the verities of Sacred Scripture."[29]

In his *Essay on the Development of Doctrine*, Newman speaks of this quality shared by the saintly Doctors and theologians of the Church: "This is a characteristic which will become more and more evident to us, the more we look for it. The divines of the Church are in every age engaged in regulating themselves by Scripture, appealing to Scripture in proof of their conclusions, and exhorting and teaching in the thoughts and language of Scripture. Scripture may be said to be the medium in which the mind of the Church has energized and developed."[30]

Theology and catechesis will not be renewed without a deliberate and wholehearted return to Scripture. In his brilliant and suggestive study on *The Roman Catechism in the Catechetical Tradition of the Church*, Robert Bradley, S.J., writes of the golden age of "classic catechesis" in the fourth and fifth century Fathers, that it "was not only Scripturally oriented but, we may say Scripturally saturated."[31] May it be said of the Church again soon.

---

[29] *The Great Commentary of Cornelius A. Lapide: Saint Matthew's Gospel*, vol. 1, trans. T. W. Mossman (Edinburgh: John Grant, 1908).

[30] John Henry Cardinal Newman, *Essay on the Development of Christian Doctrine* (Garden City, NY: Doubleday, 1960), 323.

[31] Robert I. Bradley, S.J., *The Roman Catechism in the Catechetical Tradition of the Church: The Structure of the Roman Catechism as Illustrative of the "Classic Catechesis"* (Lanham, MD: University Press of America, 1990), 57.

2. Recovery of the Fourfold Sense. If anyone should ask, "How is Scripture to be interpreted?" the text of the *Catechism* provides an answer under the heading: "The Holy Spirit, interpreter of Scripture." After reviewing three basic interpretive criteria from *Dei Verbum*, the text adds: "According to an ancient tradition, one can distinguish between two senses of Scripture: the literal and the spiritual, the latter being subdivided into the allegorical, moral and anagogical senses. The profound concordance of the four senses guarantees all its richness to the living reading of Scripture in the Church" (*Catechism*, no. 115, emphasis omitted).

It is of great significance that the four senses of Scripture found their way not only into the text of the *Catechism*, but, even more, into the section dealing with the Spirit's interpretive role. For the fourfold meaning of Scripture— sometimes referred to as typology, spiritual exegesis, or the mystical interpretation—is one of the most powerful influences in shaping Catholic theology and catechesis over the centuries.[32] Bradley offers interesting arguments showing that the fourfold structure of the classic catechesis—the Apostles' Creed, the Sacraments, the Commandments, and the Lord's Prayer—may actually be based on a reflexive imitation of the four senses of Scripture that so enamored the Fathers. This structure is reflected in both the *Catechism of the Catholic Church* and the *Catechism of the Council of*

---

[32] For a monumental work on the subject, see Henri de Lubac, *Exégèse médiévale: les quatre sens de l'Ecriture*, in 4 vols. (Paris: Aubier, 1959–64). For an English translation, see Henri de Lubac, *Medieval Exegesis: The Four Senses of Scripture*, vol.1, trans. Mark Sebanc, vol. 2, trans. E. M. Macierowski (Grand Rapids, MI: Wm. B. Eerdmans, 1998).

Trent. Further evidence of the influence of the four senses is found throughout the writings of Irenaeus, Augustine, Aquinas, Bonaventure, and countless others.

Scholars in the modern era have recognized this as well. For instance, Cardinal Newman, in his *Essay on the Development of Doctrine*—under the heading, "Scripture and Its Mystical Interpretation"—has this to say: "It may be almost laid down as an historical fact, that the mystical interpretation and orthodoxy will stand or fall together."[33] In reviewing the vast and impressive work of Henri de Lubac, S.J., Hans Urs von Balthasar examines his monumental study of medieval exegesis and the formative role played by Scripture's fourfold sense:

> [T]he theory of the sense of Scripture is not a curiosity of the history of theology but an instrument for seeking out the most profound articulations of salvation history. When Scripture is so conceived, the notion that it is sufficient for the complete interpretation of revelation, and thereby also for the construction of the whole of theology, can hold true from antiquity through the Middle Ages to the Reformation. In this it was, of course, self-evident that Scripture is read by the Church and by the individual only within the Church.[34]

Von Balthasar further notes: "For when exegesis is understood in this way, it includes all of theology, from its

---

[33] John Henry Cardinal Newman, *Essays on the Development of Christian Doctrine*, 37.
[34] Hans Urs von Balthasar, "The Achievement of Henri de Lubac," *Thought* 51 (1976): 79; reprinted as *The Theology of Henri de Lubac* (San Francisco: Ignatius, 1991), 76.

historical foundation to its most spiritual summits." Thus, he concludes that "the theology of the present and of the future will have to emulate all this."[35]

3. Re-appropriation of Spiritual Exegesis. The spiritual exegesis of Scripture is a discipline that is neither arbitrary nor disordered. In fact, it is rooted in Scripture itself, particularly as it is manifested in the interpretation of the Old Testament in the New Testament. This is confirmed by the exhaustive research of Richard M. Davidson in his dissertation, *Typology in Scripture: A Study of Hermeneutical 'Typos' Structures.* This work is a comprehensive study of every single example of an explicit Old Testament "type" treated by New Testament writers. Interestingly, Davidson writes within the strong anti-Catholic tradition of Seventh Day Adventism, with little awareness of patristic and medieval exegesis. Nevertheless, from studying the New Testament treatment of Old Testament types, he discovers a fourfold interpretive framework that is practically identical to the typology of the medieval Quadriga. At the end of his study, he concludes:

> Our discussion thus far has pointed to a fourfold salva-tion-historical substructure for the New Testament writers: (1) The historical rule of God in the period of the patriarchs and national Israel; (2) the basic fulfillment of the Old Testament eschatological hopes centered in the first advent of Jesus Christ; (3) the (derived) spiritual fulfillment by the Church in the time of tension between the "already" and the "not yet"; and (4) the apocalyptic consummation and ushering in of the Age to Come.[36]

---

[35] Balthasar, "The Achievement of Henri de Lubac," 79, 81.
[36] Richard M. Davidson, *Typology in Scripture: A Study of Hermeneutical 'Typos' Structures* (Berrien Springs, MI: Andrews University Press, 1981), 393.

Curiously, Emil Brunner also recognizes the parallels between the New Testament writers' handling of Scripture and the Catholic tradition of spiritual exegesis—a practice which he promptly rejects and warns others against:

> To argue that it is right to use typology as exposition because it was used by the Apostles is an argument that would only enter the head of a Fundamentalist. For him the whole Bible is God's infallible oracle, and all that the Apostles say has equal divine authority. This unfortunate confusion of thought . . . can only be described by the word "terrible." We can only warn people most urgently against this confusion of thought, which inevitably leads us back to a religious position which the Reformers had overcome; indeed, this victory constituted the Reformation.[37]

Here we have a profound and succinct summary of three critical points. First, there is a superficial resemblance between the Catholic and fundamentalist view of Scripture; for both, Scripture is divinely inspired and infallible. Second, those who hold this view of Scripture look to the biblical writers as exegetical guides, but only the Catholic follows their interpretive example. In other words, Scripture's divine inspiration and inerrancy imply a hermeneutic that Catholics accept, but Fundamentalists refuse. Third, Protestantism

---

[37] Emil Brunner, *The Christian Doctrine of Creation and Redemption* (Philadelphia: Westminster, 1952), 213.

is constituted by the rejection of the typological interpretation of Scripture that Catholics derived from the
New Testament writers themselves. In sum, Catholic tradition takes a more biblical approach to the Bible than
so-called Bible Christians.

Judging from exegetical and historical perspectives,
Brunner is absolutely correct in asserting that the
Catholic tradition of spiritual exegesis is based on
Scripture, just as he accurately describes how
Protestantism abandoned the spiritual sense and absolu-
tized the literal. What is fascinating is how Brunner truly
sees in Catholics more than they see in themselves.
Ironically, in the process, Brunner underscores what is
perhaps the most significant difference between how
Scripture is used by Catholics and Fundamentalists.
Unfortunately, there are Catholic exegetes who remain
oblivious to this profound difference as well; some even
follow Brunner.

4. Let Scripture Transform Culture. While the issue of
inculturation is too vast and complex to treat adequately
here, a few suggestions regarding Scripture's role in the
process of inculturating the Gospel may be helpful.
However, first we must define what we mean by the
process of inculturation. A good definition is offered by
the International Theological Commission in their 1988
document on *Faith and Inculturation:* "The process of
inculturation may be defined as the church's efforts to
make the message of Christ penetrate a given sociocultur-
al milieu, calling on the latter to grow according to all its
particular values, as long as these are compatible with the

Gospel."[38] This document goes on to show how Scripture offers a series of paradigms for understanding the process and problems of inculturation. First, the history of ancient Israel provides a paradigm of a nation struggling with God's free offer of a gracious covenant, which calls them to renounce sin and embrace righteousness. Second, the person of Jesus Christ offers a paradigm that teaches that "cultures, analogically comparable to the humanity of Christ in whatever good they possess, may play a positive role of mediation in the expression and extension of the Christian faith."[39] Third, the early Church presents a paradigm as well: "Scandal for the Jews, the mystery of the cross is foolishness to the pagans. Here the inculturation of the faith clashes with the radical sin of idolatry which keeps "captive" the truth of a culture which is not assumed by Christ."[40] Once again, a magisterial source points to the referential authority of Scripture for guidance. However, the important role of Scripture exceeds that of mere guidance. It is to be constantly consulted so that God's truth might penetrate us as persons and cultures.

Cardinal Congar discusses this model in the Middle Ages:

> The ideal, then, is that of a simultaneous penetration of all culture by Scripture, and of a reading of Scripture

---

[38] International Theological Commission, "Faith and Inculturation," *Origins* 18 (May 4, 1989): 802; see also F. E. George, O.M.I., *Inculturation and Ecclesial Communion: Culture and Church in the Teaching of Pope John Paul II* (Rome: Urbaniana University Press, 1990).

[39] International Theological Commission, "Faith and Inculturation," 800.

[40] International Theological Commission, "Faith and Inculturation," 804.

with all the resources of culture. This mutual penetration is such that Scripture is sovereign because, fully adapted as it is to the lowliness of our weakness, it is from heaven and makes known the absolute truth of things. The Fathers, and our Western Middle Ages, which took this outlook from Saint Augustine and Cassiodorus, realized, with what resources they had, a unity of wisdom, between all knowledge and life itself, under the sovereignty of the Bible. The preaching of the Fathers, their polemical works, those writings which we might term spiritual, all seek, by gathering together the knowledge of the soul and of the world, to be no more than an unfolding or an application of the texts of sacred Scripture.[41]

Thus, Scripture provided the key to transforming barbaric European tribes into the Western civilization more accurately called "Christendom."

Perhaps the greatest dimension of this achievement may well be the conversion and harnessing of the liberal arts tradition for the Christian faith. Perhaps nowhere else were patristic and medieval efforts at inculturation so successful as when they applied the liberal arts—especially the quadrivium—to preaching and teaching the four senses of Scripture. As Karl F. Morrison describes their strategy in his article on "Incentives for Studying the Liberal Arts": "Their task was, first, to use the arts to disclose the hidden mysteries of Scripture."[42] This is confirmed from the research of Ralph McInerny who describes it more fully:

---

[41] Yves Cardinal Congar, *Tradition and Traditions*, 66–67.
[42] Karl F. Morrison, "Incentives for Studying the Liberal Arts," in *The Seven Liberal Arts in the Middle Ages*, ed. D. L. Wagner (Bloomington, IN: Indiana University Press, 1986), 38.

First, the standard way of regarding the liberal arts entailed from the beginning that they were viewed as propaedeutic, instrumental, *viae* to something else. Second, this something else in the early Middle Ages tended to be identified with the wisdom contained in Scripture. One wanted to study the liberal arts in order to be a better, more adroit reader of Holy Writ. . . . [I]n the earlier period, efforts to secularize the study of the arts, that is, to divorce them from their orientation to Scripture, were regarded as dangerous by such men as Hugh of Saint Victor.[43]

Those who taught the liberal arts became, for all practical purposes, medieval Catholic missionaries to a pagan culture. They are largely responsible, then, for bringing to fruition the process of cultural death and resurrection for Europe, through teaching and preaching the wisdom of Christ in Scripture. As R. E. McNally states:

For both monk and schoolman, the Bible was the *regina scientiarum* [queen of the sciences], not only because it continued God's inspiration and revelation, but also because it was the deposit of all true wisdom and piety, the focus of all true education and learning. Its exegesis was an almost infinite task because of its *mira profunditas*, that wondrous profundity which scarcely any man could ever fathom. But the exegete's progressive uncovering of this profound deposit of truth made possible the progressive development of dogma. Education was ordered to preparing the exegete; and the task of exegesis, the interpretation

---

[43] Ralph McInerny, "Beyond the Liberal Arts," in *The Seven Liberal Arts in the Middle Ages*, 257, italics omitted.

of Scripture, coincided with the task of theology. Up to the end of the 13th century the terms *theologia* and *Sacra Scriptura* coalesced in meaning. This is illustrated by the way these expressions were used interchangeably. [44]

What a challenge this presents to Catholics facing the second death and possible extinction of the West! Our task is nothing less than the re-evangelization and re-inculturation of a society that is post-Christian and anti-Catholic. For that, nothing less than the inspired wisdom of God will suffice. If we wonder where to start, the example of the early Fathers points to the power and the place: preaching Scripture from the pulpit. As John Paul II urges: "Preaching, centered upon the Bible texts, must then in its own way make it possible to familiarize the faithful with the whole of the mysteries of the faith and with the norms of Christian living. Much attention must be given to the homily: it should be neither too long nor too short; it should always be carefully prepared, rich in substance and adapted to the hearers, and reserved to ordained ministers" (*CT*, 48).

Listen closely to Mother Church; she is calling Catholics to become Bible Christians—and Bible Christians to become Catholics!

---

[44] R. E. McNally, "Medieval Exegesis," *New Catholic Encyclopedia*, vol. 5 (New York: McGraw-Hill, 1967), 709, italics and citations in original. McNally continues: "Thus St. Thomas Aquinas (d. 1274) wrote: *"Haec est theologia quae sacra scriptura dicitur"* (*In Boeth. de Trin.* 5.4), and Saint Bonaventure: "Sacra scriptura quae theologia dicitur" *(Breviloquium. Prologus).*

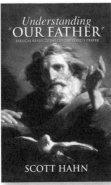

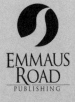

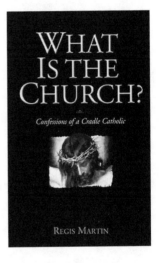